Working in the Twenty - First Century

Michael Moynagh
&
Richard Worsley

ECONOMIC & SOCIAL RESEARCH COUNCIL

THE TOMORROW PROJECT

Published by the Economic & Social Research Council, Future of Work Programme, Western Campus, University of Leeds, Leeds LS2 9JT and The Tomorrow Project, PO Box 160, Burnham Norton, King's Lynn, Norfolk PE31 8GA .

Design, editing, typesetting and production by OPS Limited, Leeds.

ISDN No: 0-9541278-1-1

Economic & Social Research Council,
Future of Work Programme,
Western Campus,
University of Leeds,
Leeds LS2 9JT

Tel: 0113 343 4504
Website: www.leeds.ac.uk/esrcfutureofwork

PO Box 160, Burnham Norton,
King's Lynn,
Norfolk PE31 8GA

Tel: 01328 730297
Website: www.tomorrowproject.net

Registered charity no. 1087016

Contents

Acknowledgements, Foreword & Commentary

1. Introduction: the main themes.   1

What work will be available?   5

2. How many jobs will there be?   7

3. What will be the quality of these jobs?   19

4. What skills will these jobs require?   27

Who will do this work?   35

5. More older workers?   37

6. More workers from abroad?   47

7. More workers from the edge of the labour market?   59

8. Better opportunities for women?   71

How will work be organised?   83

9. Will people work for themselves?   85

10. Is the 'end of jobs for life' a myth?   93

11. Will home-working take off?   101

12. How will organisations change?   111

How will work be managed?   125

13. Will workers be empowered or controlled?   127

14. How will employees be rewarded?   137

15. Do trade unions have a future?   149

What balance will be struck between work and 'life'?   161

16. Will people spend less time at work?   163

17. Flexibility for whom?   171

18. Conclusion   183

Selected bibliography   186

Index   191

Acknowledgements

We are grateful to Dr Averil Horton for compiling many of the statistics, and to the following who commented on the emerging text: Mike Emmott, Dr John Knell, Professor Bruce Lloyd, Pamela Meadows, Professor Peter Nolan and David Yeandle. Remaining shortcomings are of course ours. We are especially grateful for the encouragement and practical support provided by the ESRC's Future of Work Programme.

Michael Moynagh and Richard Worsley,
June 2005

Foreword

Working in the 21st Century by Michael Moynagh and Richard Worsley is a timely and challenging contribution to contemporary debates about the changing world of work. Unlike many other commentaries that rely on anecdotes and speculation to form judgements about work futures, this study is firmly rooted in the evidence base. It draws upon the latest research produced by social scientists, particularly from the ESRC Future of Work Programme.

The authors - an academic and senior practitioner – are leading experts in forward looking research in the UK, and have directed the highly successful Tomorrow Project that has spawned many crucial interventions into social, political and economic debates.

The present book asks large questions about how work is developing. What will employment be like in the future? Will present trends that include the decline of manufacturing industries and the growth of the service sector continue? Presently in the UK one in eight employees is engaged in services. Many work in low-paid, low-status jobs in the caring services, hotel and catering and retail. The remaining sections of manufacturing remain vital to the prosperity of the UK economy and support many of the services that have grown in recent decades. Manufacturing industries have been declining in the UK for many years, but decline is not inevitable as developments in China, for example, demonstrate.

How will this complex interplay of economic dynamics play-out in the next two decades? Will services yield the high value added employment opportunities or centre on more low-paid, low-status and part time job opportunities for, among others, the expanding student population? Or are UK employers poised to develop new business practices that will result in more training and investment in basic skills to lift performance and pay?

What are the prospects for employment relations? Declining union membership and influence in the workplaces of the UK has deprived many employees of an effective voice mechanism. New management practices focusing on individual performance may have heightened the uncertainty and stress that many employees experience and report in national surveys. What is the future for trade unions and how will management respond to the representation gap in the majority of workplaces?

Will there be sufficient demand for paid employees, or will there be a shortage of suitably qualified people to work in our expanding services (health and education, for example)? Will the expanding population of university graduates succeed in finding challenging and satisfying jobs?

Recent studies suggest that the balance between paid employment and unpaid work may be changing. But the research is drawing on the changes of the recent past. How will the boundaries change between paid and un-paid work in the future, and what are the implications for work-life balance? These are merely some of the questions that Michael Moynagh and Richard Worsley address in this scrupulous interrogation of the most advanced research findings for many decades. It is a book that all stakeholders in the future world of work will need to read and reflect on.

Peter Nolan
Director, ESRC Future of Work Programme

Commentary by Rita Donaghy,

Chair of
Advisory, Concillation and Arbitration Service (Acas)

The report continues the excellent record of the Future of Work Programme in making research findings available to policy makers and practitioners in an accessible and useful form. Especially valuable is that it goes to the heart of the question implicit in the overall programme. It really does attempt to tell us about the future of work. It also raises many of the key implications that policy makers and practitioners will have to grapple with. Moreover, it does so on the basis of a massive amount of research evidence. This evidence is also qualitative as well as quantitative – it doesn't just rely on econometric evidence as so many studies do these days.

I take my hat off to Michael Moynagh and Richard Worsley for the excellent job they've done. I have no hesitation in suggesting that their report will be an indispensable resource as well as the starting point for serious discussion and debate about policy.

The questions the report asks are the challenging ones that many of us know we should be asking but which we all too often put off, namely:

What work will be available?

Who will do this work?

How will work be organised?

How will work be managed?

What balance will be struck between work and 'life'

Overall, the report is relatively optimistic in the answers it gives. Although Britain's 'hour-glass' economy will remain, workplaces will be transformed as more and more companies will be forced to increase their products' sophistication. Demand for labour will continue to grow, with relatively tight labour markets driving attempts to boost the labour supply – from among older people, immigrants, women with children and those on the edge of the labour market. Relationship skills will be at a premium. Predictions forecasting radical changes in the nature of the employment contract are unlikely to be realised. Instead, continuing today's trend, we will become steadily more flexible in the way we work, the significant trend being to 'working on the move'. Individual employees will be given greater discretion as organisations decentralise. The experience of work will also gradually be transformed with increasing attention focusing on winning commitment so that we will want to achieve the organisation's goals.

There are very important qualifications, however, especially in the sections dealing with how organisations will change and work will be managed. Competitive pressures, technology and customer relations will encourage greater decentralisation. Worries about risk, though, will seriously weaken the delegation of authority. As research is already showing, where workers have assumed new responsibilities and have had more involvement in work organisation, managers have sought new forms of control over outcomes through rigorous performance targets, peer monitoring, frequent appraisals and other forms of surveillance.

Management capacity will also prove a barrier to change. In the authors' words,

> 'Turning senior and middle managers into coaches, motivators and enablers will be a huge task. So too will be designing feedback, self-monitoring and incentive systems that will enable individuals to self-manage their work and lead change from the bottom. Middle managers may resist the empowerment of workers below them lest they lose influence.'

Perhaps the most telling point of all, though, is that none of the suggested trends will be automatic. Outcomes will depend on the choices that are made. Moreover, the choices of policy makers will be as important as the decisions of individuals – it is going to be very difficult in the light of the evidence presented here for policy makers to argue that there is no alternative to what they are proposing. One can't ask for anything more.

Rita Donaghy

1. Introduction: the main themes

> • Working in the 21st Century is an evidence-based look at the future of work in the UK over the next 20 years.
>
> • Four themes are central – moving up the value chain, tight labour markets, more change in how people work than in how they are employed and new management techniques.

Jobs are so pivotal to our lives that the future of work ought to remain high on the agenda. Individuals, organisations and government will be profoundly affected by what happens in the workplace. Yet whether and how work will be 'redefined' in Britain is still hotly debated.

In the late 1990s it was fashionable to write about the 'new economy', alternatives to full-time salaried employment, the end of 'jobs for life', the rise of the 'virtual organisation' and the expansion of homeworking.[1]

Today a more nuanced view has begun to emerge.[2] On current trends, the demand for 'knowledge' workers will grow, but so too will the pool of low-paid jobs. Temporary and part-time work will be significant, but full-time paid employment will remain dominant. Long-term careers with an employer are far from over. The virtual organisation will be one of many different types of organisation. Work will not move from the office to the home: it will often shift from one location to multiple locations.

This emerging view has highlighted the need for evidence-based approaches to the future of work. Many of the generalisations in the late 1990s have been unpicked by detailed research, which has dissolved neat trends into a complex picture.

The aim of the book

Working in the Twenty First Century seeks to tell this more complicated story. It is written for people in management, trade unions, government, research, education and the professions who want to increase their understanding of the workplace or need to make policy affecting it.

Drawing on extensive research conducted under the ESRC's Future of Work Programme and other sources, *Working in the Twenty-First Century* describes recent British trends in work, assesses whether they are likely to continue over the next 20 years and draws out some of the implications. It covers 16 themes (which are not exhaustive) from the demand for work, to how that demand might be met, to how workers will be organised, to how they will be managed (including the role of trade unions), to the work-life balance.

---

[1] For example Valerie Bayliss, *Redefining Work: An RSA Initiative,* London: RSA, 1998.
[2] For example Peter Nolan & Stephen Wood, 'Mapping the Future of Work', *British Journal of Industrial Relations*, 41(2), 2003, pp. 165-74.

This trend analysis has the advantage of rooting judgements about the future firmly in evidence. For each theme, a description of recent and current trends comes first. This provides the starting-point for assessing whether these trends are likely to continue or change.

A second stage is based on the drivers behind the current trends, whether any of these drivers are likely to strengthen or weaken and what new drivers might come into play. Being explicit about these drivers demonstrates the basis on which judgements about the future are being made.

The third stage addresses the 'so what?' question. Anticipation is essential to plan ahead. Perhaps just as important, thinking about the future can provide insights into the present. Understanding what will influence tomorrow throws light on what is shaping today. So considering the implications of what is in the pipeline, and making connections with other trends, forms an important part of the book.

Anticipating the future is always provisional. What seems to be a clear trend can be negated by a new set of data. It is easy to miss movements in the undergrowth that will spring into the open later. The future is full of surprises. This study is not therefore a one-off, but is intended to be repeated regularly, allowing perspectives on the future of work to be updated in the light of the most recent research. The compass can be constantly reset.

The main themes

Four themes for the next 20 years emerge from the current study.

Workplaces will be transformed as the British economy moves up the value chain into activities that yield higher revenue. Competition from lower cost producers in Eastern Europe, the Far East and elsewhere will not only intensify, but affect products of increasing sophistication. More and more companies will be forced to take their products into specialist, higher-value markets or develop new ones.

The workplace will be an arena of constant change as new processes are introduced, technology becomes more advanced, workers are retrained, new forms of organisation emerge and new management techniques are developed. In one sense this will be just the continuation of recent trends. But as change accelerates, the transformation in the content of jobs and how they are managed will be more profound.

This does not mean that less-skilled workers will transform into high-earning knowledge workers. Britain's 'hour-glass' shaped economy will remain. Affluent workers at the top of the glass will continue to buy restaurant, care and other services from people on low pay at the bottom.

In the middle will be jobs most at risk from technological advance and overseas competition. Will individuals who would have done these jobs trade up into better-paid occupations, perhaps putting a brake on pay increases at the higher end? Or will they trade down, depressing wages among the low-skilled?

Tight labour markets will impact many aspects of work, and will contrast with the 'end of work' predictions made when unemployment was high. In the mid 1990s the UK crossed the threshold from a period of high unemployment to an era of labour scarcity, changing the landscape radically.

Long-term prospects for the global and UK economies are quite bullish, which will keep the demand for labour robust. Even so, it would be foolhardy to bet on a continuation of Britain's uninterrupted run of growth since 1992.

An occasional recession is almost inevitable, brought about perhaps by higher commodity prices or unexpected disasters. Labour markets are likely to slacken from time to time – and may turn down sharply toward the end of our 20-year time frame: the further out to the future we go, the more climate change casts a shadow over the world's economic performance.

Despite these caveats, it would be surprising if the British economy grew at a slower average rate over most of the next two decades than during the past two. Growth at this pace would create considerable extra demand for skills.

In addition, technology will allow workers to undertake more complex tasks, requiring them to pool their skills and work collaboratively. Far from wiping jobs away, technology will inject a dose of labour intensity into many occupations. Labour-intensive, customer-facing jobs will become increasingly important. The demand for labour will continue to grow.

So too will the need to improve the quality of social capital, not least workers' relationship skills. As human interactions become more central to work, organisations employing individuals who work well together will secure a competitive advantage. Will 'emotional literacy' become a priority for the education system?

As the demand for labour expands, the supply will be squeezed. More older workers will be ready to retire while fewer young people will take full-time jobs – larger numbers will stay in education. A long history of low skills, especially in the West Midlands and the North, will contribute to skill bottlenecks.

Tight labour markets will drive attempts to boost the labour supply – from among older people, immigrants, those on the edge of the labour market and women with children. Skill famines will influence how work is organised and managed. They will temper the power of mobile capital: having invested in Britain, employers will have to listen to workers to secure their skills. But might skill shortages become so acute that investors are forced elsewhere?

Change will be more dramatic in how people work than in how they are employed. During the 1990s Charles Handy and others forecast a revolution in the nature of the employment contract. Standard, full-time, paid employment would give way to part-time work, temporary employment, portfolio working and self-employment. But this revolution has yet to materialise.

More significant will be changes in how people work. The content of jobs will alter as technology creates new possibilities. Continuing today's trend, employees will work more flexibly. Flexible employment contracts, such as temporary employment, will be less vital for organisational success than flexible working practices. Indeed, workers will often need long-term employment to accumulate the knowledge to work in smarter ways.

New methods of working will include the substantial expansion of mobile work. The trend to more homeworking per se will be less significant than working on the move – in a motorway service station, while waiting for a train, at the airport or in a hotel. Individuals will find that the office will be just one of several work locations. Formal working time may gradually fall, but fluid boundaries between work and 'life' will encourage growing numbers to work long hours informally.

Greater discretion will mean that more will be expected of employees. Often delegation will occur as organisations struggle to combine decentralisation with appropriate control. Managing this tension will remain a dominant theme, and will give rise to a variety of organisational forms. As reorganisation continues apace, changes in the content of work will be matched by rapid changes in the context of work.

New motivational forms of management will gradually transform the experience of work. Managers will seek new methods of control as they give workers more autonomy. Existing techniques will be modified, perhaps through innovative forms of electronic monitoring. But increasingly attention will focus on winning commitment so that workers want to achieve the organisation's goals.

The shift from protecting workers through collective agreements to protection through statutory rights may reinforce the spread of motivational management. Risks of litigation already loom large for employers, and concerns will grow. Managers may want to win 'the hearts and minds' of workers to help avoid litigation.

Organisations will increase employee involvement in workplace decisions, seek to align their values to those of employees and broaden the concept of reward. Reward will come to mean much more than an extensive 'menu' from which individuals can compile their remuneration packages. It will include the physical environment of work, a supportive management style and other elements that can help jobs become a source of well-being.

Managers wedded to hierarchies will not take naturally to these new approaches. But in the long-term younger generations, steeped in an 'open source' culture, will embrace 'bottom-up' forms of organisation and seek management methods to match. How well equipped will they be to lead the change?

What work will be available?

2. How many jobs will there be?

- Jobs have reached a record number as the UK has moved up the value chain and certain aspects of work have become more labour-intensive.

- Job openings will expand further as the economy grows, the shift to interpersonal work turns this growth into employment and existing workers leave their jobs.

- The growing demand for workers will keep labour markets tight, exert a major influence on the workplace and make work more central to people's lives.

Around the mid 1990s a sea-change occurred in the British economy. Before then unemployment had been one of Britain's top political issues. Since then skill shortages have spread.

High unemployment in the 1980s and early '90s sparked fears that advancing technology and competition from low-wage producers abroad would destroy jobs in the advanced world. Washington-based environmentalist, Jeremy Rifkin, was one of several commentators to write about the 'End of Work'.[1] There would be nowhere near enough jobs for those who wanted them.

Yet prolonged economic growth since 1992 has created an unprecedented number of jobs. A record number of people are in work today, and unemployment is lower than at any time since the 1970s. Many sectors face skill shortages. Will the economy continue to generate plenty of jobs, or might recent trends be an interlude between one period of job scarcity and another?

The story so far

Global competition is pushing the economy higher up the value chain, creating jobs in the process.

'The UK currently faces a transition to a new phase of economic development...We find that the competitiveness agenda facing UK leaders in government and business reflects the challenges of moving from a location competing on relatively low costs of doing business to a location competing on unique value and innovation.

---

[1] Jeremy Rifkin, *The End of Work,* New York: Putnam, 1995. Rifkin repeated this view in *The Guardian,* 2 March 2004.

> This transition requires investments in different elements of the business environment, upgrading of company strategies, and the creation and strengthening of new types of institutions.'[2]

Many 'low-cost' jobs in mining and manufacturing, in which the UK was unable to compete, disappeared in the 1980s and '90s – and have continued to do so since. For example, UK imports of refrigerators from China jumped from zero in 1995 to 998,500 units in 2003, just over 38% of all fridge imports.[3]

But jobs adding greater value per employee have increased in activities where Britain has a competitive advantage, such as financial and professional services and the 'creative' industries (which were the second largest generator of jobs in London between 1995 and 2000[4]). Marketing staff, advertising agencies, packaging designers, photographers and a string of consultants en route account for a much larger proportion of the retail price of an 'imported' product than the manufacturing costs abroad.

The race up the value chain has been led by London, where the switch from manufacturing and back office jobs to business and creative occupations has pushed up gross value added per head faster than in other regions.[5]

Chart 2.1 shows recent employment trends by sector, based on the 1991 and 2001 census data. Banking and finance, and – a little surprisingly – transport[6] were the two fastest growing industries. The largest single industry in 2001 was distribution and catering. The significant growth of 'other services' was largely due to the expansion of employment in health and education.

---

[2] M. E. Porter & C. H. M. Ketels, 'UK Competitiveness: Moving to the Next Stage', *DTI Economics Paper No. 3,* London: DTI/ESRC, 2003, Introduction.

[3] Theo Nichols, 'Internationalisation of the white goods sector: implications for management and labour', paper presented to *Future of Work: 2nd International Colloquium,* Leeds, 9-10 Sept. 2004.

[4] Michael Moynagh & Richard Worsley, *Learning from the future: Scenarios for post-16 learning,* London: Learning & Skills Research Centre, 2003, p. 21.

[5] *Regional Futures: England's Regions in 2030,* London: ODPM & DfT, 2005, p. 13.

[6] Unconventionally, Dorling and Thomas do not include 'communications' (such as telecoms/internet) alongside transport as a single category. Presumably, 'communications' is lumped in with 'other services', though this is not explicitly stated.

Chart 2.1 UK employment trends by sector 1991-2001

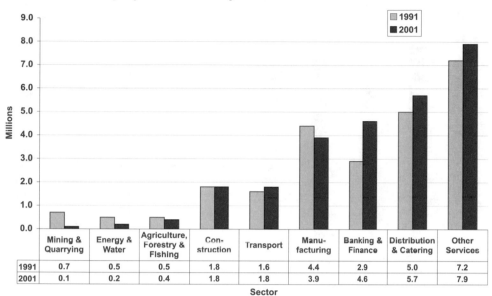

	Mining & Quarrying	Energy & Water	Agriculture, Forestry & Fishing	Con-struction	Transport	Manu-facturing	Banking & Finance	Distribution & Catering	Other Services
1991	0.7	0.5	0.5	1.8	1.6	4.4	2.9	5.0	7.2
2001	0.1	0.2	0.4	1.8	1.8	3.9	4.6	5.7	7.9

Sector

Source: Daniel Dorling & Bethan Thomas, *People and Places: A 2001 Census atlas of the UK*, Bristol: Policy Press, 2004, pp. 116-24.

This gradual if painful adjustment has helped the UK experience an unprecedented period of continuous economic growth since 1992, which has been the basis for employment growth as well - from a low of 25.5 million workers in 1994 to 28.4 million in 2004 (see Chart 2.3 on p.11).

The restructuring of the UK economy has increased the demand for labour-intensive activities. Restructuring has helped the economy become more prosperous, which has enabled people to spend more in the shops and on personal and other services, most with a high labour content.

Chart 2.2 shows that during the 1990s 'associate professionals' experienced a faster increase relatively than any other occupation. Many of these were nurses, social workers or were employed in the police and fire services. Labour-intensive 'elementary occupations', such as shelf-stacking in retail and cleaning in the service sector, had the second fastest growth.

'Personal services' showed a significant decline, even though hairdressing was the fastest growing occupation in Britain.[7] But this decline was almost entirely offset by the expansion of 'sales and customer service'. 'Professionals', dominated by health and education, grew substantially.

---

[7] Peter Nolan & Gary Slater, 'The Labour Market: History, Structure and Prospects' in Paul Edwards (ed), *Industrial Relations. Theory and Practice,* Oxford: Blackwell, 2003, p. 66.

Chart 2.2 UK employment trends by occupation 1991-2001

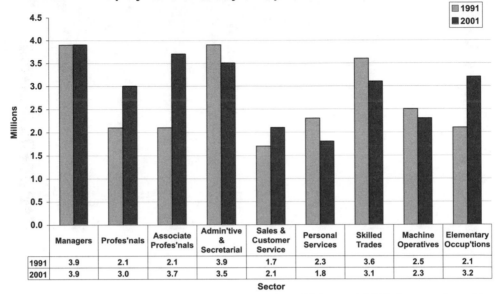

	Managers	Profes'nals	Associate Profes'nals	Admin'tive & Secretarial	Sales & Customer Service	Personal Services	Skilled Trades	Machine Operatives	Elementary Occup'tions
1991	3.9	2.1	2.1	3.9	1.7	2.3	3.6	2.5	2.1
2001	3.9	3.0	3.7	3.5	2.1	1.8	3.1	2.3	3.2

Sector

Source: Daniel Dorling & Bethan Thomas, *People and Places*: *A 2001 Census atlas of the UK*, Bristol: Policy Press, 2004, pp. 107-115

Human interactions are a growing component of many jobs, even where they are not customer-facing. In the past, relationships were often secondary to the job. Friendships were formed at work, but they were a background to the job: tasks frequently required little interaction with people. Notices would appear, 'Less talk, more work!'

Pin that up today and it would look anachronistic. That is because there has been a revolution in the content of many jobs. In many cases talk has become the job – 'Can I speak to so-and-so?' 'Sorry, they are in a meeting.' A 1998 London School of Economics study examined a wide range of occupations up and down the skills ladder. In nearly every case it was reported that the time spent interacting with people had increased.[8]

Technology is automating routine tasks and in some jobs makes possible more complex ones. These more complicated tasks are often beyond the skills of any one person, which is why we hear so much today about collaboration, team-work, joint ventures and interpersonal skills. In other jobs, automation allows more time for interfacing with customers or for other human interactions.

---

[8] Frances Green, David Ashton, Brendan Burchell, Bryn Davies & Alan Felstead, 'Are British Workers Getting More Skilled?' in A. B. Atkinson & John Hills, *Exclusion, Employment and Opportunity,* London: LSE Centre for Analysis of Social Exclusion, 1998, pp. 89-131.

Far from dispensing with people as Rifkin and other predicted, technology has introduced a new element of labour intensity into many jobs. Middle managers, with the labour-intensive task of supervising others, comprised almost a third of the rapidly growing 'associate professionals' category in 2001.

The result of these developments is that there are more jobs in Britain, and more people in employment, than ever before. Chart 2.3 shows how total employment fell from a peak in 1979 to a low in 1983, hit another peak in 1990, declined considerably till 1994 and has risen since to a record 28.4 million. Paid work has an unprecedented place in people's lives.

Chart 2.3 Numbers in employment (UK, all 16 and over, seasonally adjusted, annual)

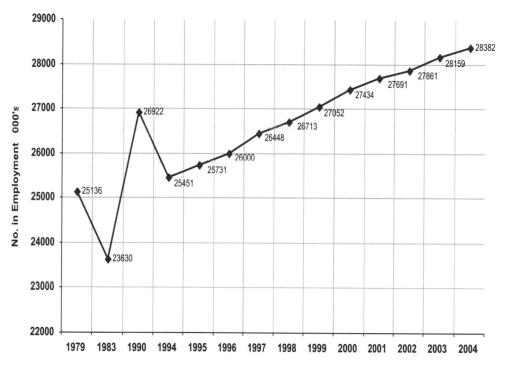

Source: ONS Labour Market Statistics – Integrated FR LFS TIME PERIODS, Table MGRZ.

The next 20 years

Global economic growth will form a platform for more jobs in Britain. Drivers propelling this growth will include:[9]

- falling transport and communication costs due to technology, which will facilitate the further expansion of world trade – between 1970 and 1999 the cost of one megahertz of processing power fell from $7,601 to 17 cents;

- the expansion of foreign direct investment (FDI), which will increase the world's productive potential – world FDI flows expanded by an average of 13% p.a. between 1990 and 1997, and accelerated to an unprecedented average of almost 50% a year from 1998 to 2000;

- the greater specialisation and internationalisation of production (reflected in the expansion of 'offshoring'), which will make the world economy more efficient and so increase its capacity to grow;

- the increasing importance of China and India as engines of the global economy – the Chinese and Indian economics have grown by over 700% and 250% since 1980. Assuming political stability, by 2015 China is likely to have become the world's third largest economy after the US and Japan. About half China's 800 million rural population may have little work to do in the coming decades as its agriculture approaches current Western levels of efficiency. Despite shortages of managerial and other skills, this could keep down the real wages of unskilled and semi-skilled labour, and allow China to expand industrial production phenomenally without pricing itself out of world markets.[10]

Against these bullish prospects is the risk that tight energy supplies, for example, mismanagement of the US or Chinese economies or a major disaster will threaten world economic growth and stifle job creation in Britain. The further out we go to the mid 2020s, the greater is the danger that climate change will cast a shadow over the global economy.

---

[9] This paragraph is based on HM Treasury, *Long-term global economic challenges and opportunities for the UK,* London: The Stationery Office, 2004, ch. 2.
[10] Roger Bootle, *Money for Nothing. Real Wealth, Financial Fantasies, and the Economy of the Future,* London: Nicholas Brealey, 2004, p. 148.

On balance however, the world is likely to see strong overall economic growth, despite knocks from time to time. Based on World Bank projections, the international economy could balloon by 40% between 2005 and 2015.[11]

The UK economy is well-placed to take advantage of this global growth. International markets will expand for many of the things that Britain does well – for example:

- business services, such as accounting and legal and advisory work;

- health and education (especially pharmaceuticals and university education[12]);

- hi-tech manufacturing like aerospace, and the craft end of manufacturing, such as luxury boat-building, which collectively is quite large.[13]

- earnings from rights, royalties, licence payments, brands, overseas investments and the like, which should remain substantial. [14]

Based on Eurostat figures, so-called knowledge-intensive sectors account for 41% of employment in Britain, higher than in France, Germany, Italy and Spain, and well above the EU average of 33%. These sectors tend to be the fastest growing parts of the economy, and have been key to Britain's growth outstripping the 'euroland' countries for 11 years in a row.[15]

Investors will continue to value the UK's robust framework for macro-economic policy, underpinned by the Bank of England's independence in setting interest rates, which should help maintain stability and low inflation. Britain's comparatively healthy public finances (despite immediate concerns) should be under less pressure than our main European competitors, who have larger state pension commitments to their ageing populations, and this will make Britain relatively attractive to business. High-quality education at the top end will appeal to investors further up the value chain.

---

[11] HM Treasury, *Long-term global economic challenges,* op. cit., p. 22.

[12] The global education market is huge: more than 500,000 international students enrolled at American universities in 1999-2000. Roger Bootle, *op. cit.,* London: Nicholas Brealey, 2003, p. 362.

[13] Britain was one of the very few advanced economies to maintain its share of world exports in the 1990s (at 5.2%), despite sterling's real exchange rate rising significantly after mid 1996. M.E. Porter & C.H.M. Ketels, *op. cit.,* ch.2.

[14] In 2002 royalties and licence fees accounted for some 6% of the UK's total service exports, and for the US 15% ($43 billion). Between 1986 and 2002 the world's service exports grew by some 230%, but earnings from fees and licences grew by 430%. Profits from direct investment abroad account for over 10% of all income accruing to the US and UK. Roger Bootle, *op. cit.,* p. 227.

[15] David Smith, 'Sun shines on UK prospects', *The Sunday Times,* 20 March 2005.

But it would be rash to ignore the danger signals – not least, the possibility that the terms of trade will turn against Britain. In recent years, manufacturing import prices have been comparatively stable and are now falling. At the same time, the value of goods and services produced within the UK and often exported has continued to rise – an increase that in a low inflation age has contributed to higher retail prices (Chart 2.4).

These favourable terms of trade have added to Britain's wealth. A London-based engineer might earn 50% more for his services overseas than 10 years ago (without any increase in productivity), but pay less for his imported clothes and new car.

Chart 2.3 *Movements in manufacturing import prices and retail prices 1998-2004*

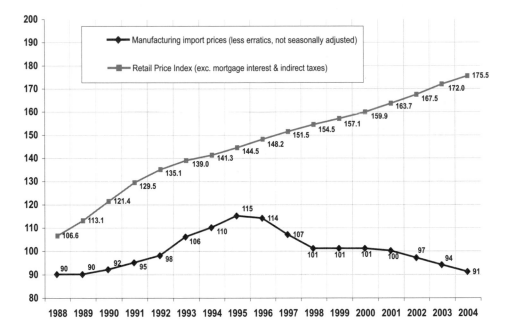

Source: ONS Time Series, Trade in Goods MRETS, Tables ELAX, CBZW.

But will this healthy position last? Britain could face mounting competition in areas where she has traditional strengths, such as financial and business services, as other countries develop their expertise.

Emerging and developing economies are starting to chase the more industrialised world up the value chain. Between the early 1980s and early 2000s, high-tech manufacturing growth averaged 5.5% in the more developed economies, but 9.3% in the emerging and developing ones.[16]

When a worldwide sample of senior executives was asked in 2004 where they would spend the most on R & D in the next three year, 39% said China, 29% the US, 28% India, 24% the UK and 19% Germany.[17] The popularity of China and India is striking. It cannot be long before both countries climb the value chain not only in manufacturing, but in financial and business services too.

Britain is already running a substantial current account deficit. Correcting this in the long-term may not be easy. The UK economy is heavily dependent on the sluggish EU rather than blazing inroads into fast-growing China and India.[18] Is Britain economically too close to the wrong countries? Chicago boasts 3000 students in its state schools who are learning Mandarin.[19] Is Britain gearing up to China to the same extent?

Compounding the export challenge will be the loss of Britain's self-sufficiency in oil by 2007 and soon after in gas. As the UK becomes an oil and gas importer, sterling will lose its petro-currency status and its value may well fall. This could be quite a painful adjustment. Might interest rates rise to curb the inflationary effects of sterling's depreciation?

In the long run, a lower pound would increase the competitiveness of British business. But in the short term growth could stall, confidence suffer and import prices rise, effectively reducing national wealth. Joining the euro at a high exchange rate before this adjustment was complete would slow economic and employment growth still further, perhaps for a prolonged period.

Despite these challenges, the unprecedented length of Britain's recent economic growth suggests the economy has strengths that bode well for the future. These strengths probably outweigh the dangers, which will allow the jobs total to balloon over the long-term. But the path will be uneven. There will be times when the economy slows, the flight of jobs abroad exceeds new ones at home and unemployment rises. In other periods, labour supplies will tighten as the economy and jobs market pick up.

---

[16] HM Treasury, *Long-term global economic challenges,* op. cit., p.31.

[17] Laura Abramovsky, Rachel Griffin & Mari Sako, *Offshoring of business services and its impact on the UK economy,* London: AIM Research, 2004, p. 15.

[18] Almost 60% of UK exports go to the EU, the world's slowest growing region, while China and India, the fastest growing, receive only 1% each. Germany exports seven times as much to China as the UK. UK foreign direct investment in China and India is tiny compared to the 70% of UK investment in Europe. Christopher Smallwood, 'UK misses out on Asian boom', *The Sunday Times,* 29 August 2004.

[19] 'The battle for the Great Lakes', *The Economist,* 23 October 2004.

The shift to interpersonal work will help translate economic growth into jobs growth. The importance of human interactions in many jobs will grow as technology makes possible more advanced products and processes, requiring higher levels of co operation between workers. Improved video conferencing, virtual reality and other technologies will underpin more sophisticated forms of collaboration. As incomes rise the demand for personal, labour-intensive services will continue to expand.

Although it is common to say that we have entered the 'knowledge economy', might we be at the start of a long-term trend away from 'knowledge' workers to workers who add value through human interaction?

In the initial phase of automation, brain power tends to replace brawn power by automating a growing number of physical activities. But in time electronic and new forms of mechanical intelligence will increasingly supplement brain power with computer power. 'Intellect seems easier for computers to learn than supposedly more simple human interaction skills.'[20]

Might a time be coming when only jobs in which people are an essential component of the service, such as caring and personal services, are really safe? Differences in performance would be based on personality, warmth and emotional intelligence. This very long-term trend would make the economy – almost by definition – more labour-intensive, which would create jobs.

Long-term forecasts for the economy need to take these developments into account. Economic growth may be more labour-intensive than existing models allow.

By far the most job openings will be to replace existing workers who leave the labour force or change jobs. The Warwick Institute for Employment Research estimates that about 13.5 million job openings will be created between 2002 and 2012, of which almost 12.2 million will be replacements for existing workers. The number of new jobs will be just over 1.3 million.[21] Employment will continue to expand thereafter.

What might be the implications?

The net expansion of jobs will keep labour markets tight, together with the demographic factors discussed in chapters 5 to 8. Skill shortages will be most acute in the London 'mega-city region' and in centres like Edinburgh, Leeds and Manchester which have particular strengths.

---

[20] Ian Pearson, "The future of the Care Economy", http://www.bt.com/innovation/viewpoints/pearson/care_economy.htm.
[21] Institute for Employment Research, *Bulletin*, No. 73, 2004.

In general, the demand for jobs is set to grow considerably faster in the South than in the Midlands, the North of England and the Celtic rim – for several reasons:[22]

> • Manufacturing employment will continue to fall because of static output and productivity improvements. This will have most impact on the Midlands, and parts of the North and Scotland.

> • High-value jobs are most likely to be created in the South where Britain's R & D is concentrated, a disproportionate number of graduates live, and clusters of specialist services have a longer history and are self-reinforcing.

> • Economic regions outside the South depend more heavily on public services, whose recent growth will be difficult to sustain as government seeks to cut the number of back office public servants, and where pay tends to be lower than in the private sector.

Maybe tight labour markets will constrain growth in the South and narrow these disparities. But as we discuss later, older people, migrant workers and people who are currently inactive may also boost the labour supply. In the long run, securing a more balanced UK economy will require cities and their hinterlands outside the South to find new sources of competitive advantage. Might high-speed transport links, extending the London mega-city region northward, be developed?

Continuing job demand will be a key influence on working life in the next two decades. It is often said that globalisation has shifted the balance of power from labour to capital. The threat that a department will be offshored, perhaps even the entire operation closed, limits employees' bargaining power. While this will remain true, tight labour markets – partly reflecting employment growth – will go some way to redressing the balance.

As the economy moves up the value chain, many activities will require higher investment – in advanced IT and other physical assets, and in job-related training. Firms that have just made these investments will be reluctant to write them off. Faced with skill shortages, companies wanting to get a good return will have to listen to their workers carefully.

This will influence employer attitudes to 'family friendly' policies, the reward package, possible demands for longer holidays and other employee concerns. Shortages of cleaners, waiters and other low-paid workers may allow the National Minimum Wage to rise more rapidly, compelling employers at the bottom end to adopt higher-value, higher-skilled and higher-paid methods of production.

---

[22] *Regional Futures: England's Regions in 2030,* London: ODPM & DfT, 2005, pp. 10-24.

As has already begun to happen, tight labour markets will shift the public policy emphasis from cutting unemployment to boosting the labour supply. Immigration, persuading older workers to stay in employment and encouraging mothers back to work will become even higher priorities.

Work may become more central to people's lives. In the 1980s and early '90s part-time work grew significantly. Rifkin and others have seen this as evidence that technologically advanced economies cannot support high levels of employment: there are not enough jobs, so people are forced into part-time work.

But the increase in part-time employment has virtually levelled off (see Chart 17.5 on p. 175 in ch. 17). Part-time work exploded during the 1970s, and the rate of growth then slowed in the 1980s and early 90s. Much of this later growth was among students. Indeed, almost all the recent growth in part-time work among men is from students.[23]

In future, the growing demand for workers may encourage organisations to make full-time jobs more attractive – tasks requiring two part-time people would be undertaken by one person. Rather than allowing workers with families to go part-time, employers may seek family-friendly alternatives, such as greater freedom to work from home. At the same time, they may start offering older workers part-time jobs to persuade them to delay retirement and to keep using their skills.

Individuals in the prime of life would increasingly work full-time and more older workers would stay on part-time. People's lives would be more focused on work. Work and personal well-being would remain closely linked.

Points to take away

- Shifting to activities that add more value per employee will create jobs and be a key influence on the future.

- Human interactions at work will continue to grow in importance and make aspects of employment more labour-intensive

- Tight labour markets in many sectors, and especially around London, will have a large impact on the workplace.

---

[23] We are grateful to Pamela Meadows for pointing this out.

3. What will be the quality of these jobs?

• Good and bad jobs have polarised as the number of middling jobs has declined, creating an 'hour-glass' shaped society.

• Globalisation will tend to increase this polarisation. How far Britain moves up the value chain will influence whether middling jobs drift toward the top or bottom of the glass. Will tight labour markets in the South East and sharp rises in the minimum wage force employers at the bottom end to adopt higher-value, higher-paid methods of production?

• A widening gap between good and bad jobs would increase ill-health, encourage violent crime and damage social capital. Yet preventing and reversing job polarisation will be a huge challenge.

Critical for individuals' well-being will be the quality of work they undertake. The previous chapter suggested that plenty of jobs will be available in the next 20 years, but will they be 'good' jobs? Although there are many components of a 'good' job, in this chapter we focus on well-paid and badly paid jobs. How far will they be polarised?

The story so far

Chart 3.1 shows that the share of UK employment in the top two deciles (the best-paid jobs) grew most sharply between 1979 and 1999, with a smaller growth in the bottom decile. 'Middling' jobs have declined. The workforce has become more polarised, producing an 'hour-glass' glass shape to society.

Chart 3.1 % change in employment share by job quality decile, UK 1979-99

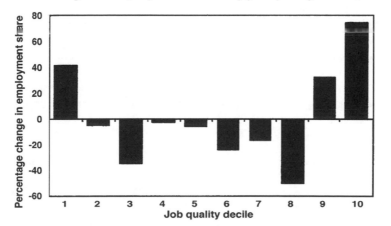

Source: Maarton Goos & Alan Manning, 'McJobs and MacJobs: The Growing Polarisation of Jobs in the UK' in Richard Dickens, Paul Gregg & Jonathan Wadsworth, *The Labour Market Under New Labour. The State of Working Britain* 2003, London: Palgrave, 2003, p. 73.

Note: Data from Labour Force Survey for 90 occupations in 10 industries.

Managers, professionals and hi-tech workers in business services and finance have swelled the number of well-paid jobs. Growing occupations at the lower-paid end have been concentrated in retail distribution, hotels and catering, and healthcare. Many of the jobs 'hollowed out' in between have been in manufacturing – mainly routine process operatives and machine operators.[1]

At the same time, the gap between top and bottom earnings has widened (See Table 3A). Workers – mostly low-paid – who did not have an occupational pension, sick pay, health insurance and other such benefits in 1992 still did not have them in 2000, while some lower-paid workers who did have one or more of these benefits no longer had them.[2]

Table 3A % change in median hourly wage rates, 1992-2000

All	5
Winners:	
Higher managers	+24
Lower managers	+11
Skilled manual	+15
Losers	
Lower professionals	-3
Semi routine	-5
Routine	-3

Source: Stephen Hill, Colin Mills & Pat McGovern, 'Inequality at work: employment conditions, harmonization and the changing workplace divide', paper presented to *Future of Work. 2nd International Colloquium*, Leeds, 9-10 Sept. 2004.

The next 20 years

Globalisation will influence the national job mix over the next two decades. As now, international competition will push up the salaries of those who are top of their fields and for whom a global market exists. The gap between the best-paid and the rest will widen.

Meanwhile, lower costs in Asia and elsewhere will continue to encourage the 'offshoring' of middling jobs, which will include a growing number in more

---

[1] The concept of the hour-glass economy is drawn from a collection of articles by Peter Nolan, Michael Moynagh and Richard Worsley in *People Management*, 27 Dec 2001.
[2] Stephen Hill, Colin Mills & Pat McGovern, 'Inequality at work: employment conditions, harmonization and the changing workplace divide', paper presented to *Future of Work. 2nd International Colloquium*, Leeds, 9-10 Sept. 2004.

skilled occupations such as equity research.[3] The labour market will hollow out still further. Automation of repetitive white collar jobs will deepen the hollow, especially in the public sector, where employment totals are due to be squeezed following the Gershon review for the Treasury of public sector efficiency.[4]

How fast and how far the UK moves up the value chain will be crucial in what happens as intermediate jobs decline. Will workers who would have filled these jobs tumble down the skills ladder in search of lower-paid work, pushing down wages nearer the bottom? Or will they scramble up to higher-skilled jobs, so that more workers bunch in better-paid occupations?

The extent of Britain's shift into higher-value activities will provide the answer. Recent trends are quite encouraging. As Chart 3.2 shows, over the last 15 years degree-level jobs have grown much faster than non-degree work (though from a low base), while jobs requiring low-level or no qualifications have declined markedly. Does this offer hope for the future?

Chart 3.2 Trends in qualifications used at work 1996-2001 (as %)

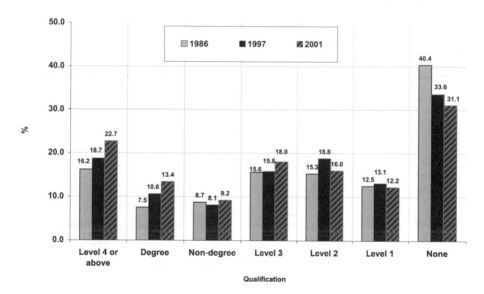

Note: 'Qualifications used' is based on data for qualifications required for the job, combined with estimates of the usefulness of qualifications once in the post.

Source: Alan Felstead, Duncan Gallie, Francis Green, *Work Skills in Britain 1986-2001*, DfES, 2002, p. 122.

---

[3] This is already beginning to happen. See for example, Chris Odino, Stephen Diacon & Christine Ennew, *Outsourcing in the UK Financial Services Industry: The Asian Offshore Market*, Nottingham: Nottingham University Business School Financial Services Research Forum, 2004, pp. 7-8.

[4] For example, it may become economic to answer routine tax and social security questions through call centres in the Far East.

Production strategies at the bottom end of the labour market will continue to trap many workers in low-value-added, low-skilled and low-paid methods of production. The 2001 Employers Skills Survey found that only 2.9 million economically active people aged 20 to 60 possessed no qualifications, but 6.5 million jobs existed for which no qualification would have been required.

'This aggregate imbalance suggests that previously reported deficiencies in Britain (by comparison with other countries) in the use of intermediate-level qualifications may be deficiencies of demand as well as of supply.'[5] Or may it be a deficiency of demand rather than supply?

Boosting skills alone is unlikely to transform organisational strategy since firms can make a profit with their existing business models. Many in retailing and other services produce for the domestic market and are unaffected by global competition. They have no incentive to change.[6] What would encourage them to move into higher-value, higher-paid methods of production?

The recent polarisation of jobs is also due to the disappearance of many unionised occupations in manufacturing and the weaker presence of unions in the lower-paid private services. Many low-paid workers have not organised to secure higher-wages.[7] Might new ways of organising them emerge?

Some developments may limit job polarisation. For example, growing demand will tighten the squeeze on many labour markets, as discussed in the last chapter. This could force some employers at the bottom end to scale down their workforces by adopting more capital-intensive methods of production, such as robotic 'hoovers' for hotel cleaning, allowing them to pay higher-wages. Or will government let employers off the hook by introducing measures to ease labour shortages, such as boosting the supply of migrant workers?

Certain public policy interventions might limit job polarisation. For example, at £4.85 an hour in October 2004, the National Minimum Wage has risen by 35% during its first five years, considerably more than for pay in general. If this trend persists, low paying employers would be compelled incrementally to adopt higher productivity and higher-skilled processes. Might this become a more explicit government strategy to combat low pay and cut the costs of in-work tax credits?

What might be the implications?

The persistence of the 'hour-glass' society will have serious long-term consequences. A continuing gulf between 'good' and 'bad' jobs is likely, and may well widen.

---

[5] *Work Skills in Britain 1986-2001,* op. cit., p. 11.

[6] Ewart Keep, Ken Mayhew, Mark Corney, *Review of the Evidence on the Rate of Return to Employers of Investment in Training and Employer Training Measures*, London: DTI, 2002, pp. 44-7.

[7] Maarton Goos & Alan Manning, 'McJobs and MacJobs: The Growing Polarisation of Jobs in the UK' in Richard Dickens, Paul Gregg & Jonathan Wadsworth, *The Labour Market Under New Labour. The State of Working Britain* 2003, London: Palgrave, 2003, p. 83.

The 'hollowing out' of intermediate jobs will make it more difficult for individuals to climb out of low-paid employment because there would be fewer rungs on the ladder to step on to. This will cement today's sizeable income gap.

Strong evidence exists that in advanced economies the size of this gap really matters. A wide gap damages the confidence of people at the bottom, undermines their self-esteem, leaves them feeling powerless and produces frustration, which can lead to physical outbursts of anger. Individuals feel anxious and isolated.

These feelings give rise to stress, which is often associated with ill-health. American states and metropolitan areas with the lowest income inequalities have the lowest mortality rates: rates are higher in states and metropolitan areas where inequality is greatest.[8]

Roseto, Pennsylvania was an unusually cohesive small town in the 1960s. Distinguishing between rich and poor neighbourhoods was difficult. Mortality rates were much lower than in nearby towns. From the 1970s incomes began to widen. Strikingly, the town lost its health advantages.[9]

Individuals at the bottom of the income pile are more likely to feel that others disrespect them – and resort to violence. A 1988 study found a strong correlation between the degree of income inequality and homicide rates. Countries with the highest inequalities had the highest homicide rates. American states with the highest inequalities had the highest homicide rates. Within 77 Chicago neighbourhoods, neighbourhoods with the highest inequalities had the highest homicide rates.[10]

Egalitarian societies appear to be more cohesive. In the USA, the proportion of people who feel they can trust others tends to be much higher in states where income differences are smaller. People in more egalitarian states find each other more helpful and are more likely to belong to voluntary clubs and associations.[11]

Much of public policy aims to improve health outcomes, reduce violent crime and increase social cohesion. But these policies are often addressing the consequences of a profoundly unequal society. A widening gap between well and badly paid jobs could put mounting strain on measures that treat the symptoms of inequality rather than the underlying causes.

The tax base needed to support these measures would be eroded if low-paid jobs were to replace most of the ones hollowed out in the middle. Might improving the quality of the bottom jobs become a priority?

---

[8] Richard G. Wilkinson, 'Putting the picture together: prosperity, redistribution, health and welfare' in Michael Marmot & Richard G. Wilkinson (eds), *Social Determinants of Health,* Oxford: OUP, 1999, p. 259.

[9] Richard Wilkinson, *Unhealthy Societies,* London: Routledge, 1996, p. 116-8.

[10] Cited by Michael Marmot, *Status Syndrome,* London: Bloomsbury, 2004, pp. 102-3.

[11] Richard Wilkinson, *Mind the Gap: Hierarchies, Health and Human Evolution,* London: Weidenfeld, 2000, p. 14.

Reversing the polarisation of Britain's labour market would be a massive challenge. UK measures to curb rises in top incomes are unlikely to be feasible – those affected would move abroad. But might preventing middle and bottom earnings from pulling further apart be a plausible goal?

Employers in the middle and at the bottom end might be encouraged to embrace higher-value methods of production to boost the demand for higher-skilled, higher-paid workers. Better jobs, closer to the middle of the earnings range, would become available to the lower-paid, narrowing the income gap.

Introducing policies to achieve this would be a significant change of direction for the UK. Despite support for small businesses and other measures, policy is still heavily skewed to improving the supply of skills rather than raising the demand.

Adopting a different tack would be risky. Effective interventions might be hard to find. Using public money (to encourage R & D for example) might prove costly and wasteful. A higher Minimum Wage – to force employers up the value chain – might be passed on in higher prices and damage the competitiveness of the hospitality industry for instance, which is vital for overseas tourism.

Even were effective measures to be found, today's success would create tomorrow's problem. Increasing the demand for higher-skilled workers at the lower end would lift the employment 'floor' further above those who were out of work, many of whom have very few skills. It would become harder to draw them in. Do policy-makers have the capacity to raise the floor and build longer ladders into work, both at the same time?

Will 'the real economy, not the new economy' become a focus of attention? The mantra is certainly an improvement on the lopsided talk about the 'new economy' and the new breed of 'knowledge' workers, which was all the rage at the turn of the millennium but which ignored the majority in less glamorous jobs.[12]

Government policy to tackle social exclusion is largely concentrated on helping people into employment. In practice this means helping them into low-paid, low quality jobs, which at best are only a partial route out of poverty – hence the various in-work tax credits, which boost the incomes of those in employment but act as an expensive form of wage subsidy.

As poverty persists despite measures to help individuals into employment, and the cost of tax credits comes under the microscope, might attention switch to turning the large number of 'McJobs' into 'good' jobs? What would it mean to have an effective national policy to improve work at the bottom end? What could a 'good' job for this section of the workforce realistically mean? Will developing and implementing a vision for 'good work' become a priority?

---

[12] Government policy focused on equipping Britain to compete in the 'knowledge economy', for example. Department of Trade and Industry, *Our Competitive Future: Building the Knowledge Driven Economy,* London: The Stationery Office, 1998.

Points to take away

• Britain's 'hour-glass' society is set to become more pronounced as jobs are hollowed out in the middle.

• Vital for the future will be whether people who would have taken these intermediate jobs trade up to better-paid employment or trade down.

• Will initiatives to increase social inclusion focus not just on getting people into work, but on improving the quality of jobs they take at the bottom end?

4. What skills will these jobs require?

• Employers' skill requirements have increased slowly, but significantly.

• The demand will grow for 'new economy' skills, especially in the so-called 'aesthetic economy', for 'old economy' skills, for interpersonal skills and for life skills.

• Employers will continue to upgrade their workers' skills, higher education will expand beyond the current target of 50% of 18 to 30 year olds, key skills will become an even higher priority and 'emotional literacy' may be included in the core curriculum.

The British economy is on a journey – as we have seen, gradually moving to more sophisticated forms of production requiring higher levels of skill, but also relying on a large 'underclass' of low-skilled jobs. Low-value products traded in the global market will face mounting competition from cheaper producers abroad. British firms will only survive by developing specialist expertise and concentrating on quality. What skills will workers require?

The story so far

Employers' skill requirements have increased slowly but significantly. The Government's national skills surveys reveal:[1]

• The proportion of jobs requiring degrees or their equivalent rose from just over 16% in 1986 to nearly 23% in 2001 (see Chart 4.1).

• Between 1997 and 2001, nine out of ten measures of generic skill showed a rise. These included literacy, number, technical know-how, problem-solving, checking, planning and various forms of communication. The exception was physical strength and/or stamina.

• The proportion of employees using computers and automated equipment increased from just over half in 1992 to almost three quarters in 2001. The importance of computer skills rose more rapidly between 1997 and 2001 than any other skill.

• More than half (53%) of managers in 2001 reported a recent increase in coaching skills, against just 7% reporting a decrease.

---

[1] This paragraph is based on Alan Felstead, Duncan Gallie, Francis Green, *Work Skills in Britain 1986-2001*, London: DfES, 2002, p. 10 & 56-7.

• The proportion of jobs requiring a cumulative training time of less than three months fell, but only modestly, from 66% in 1986 to 61% in 2001.

• The proportion of jobs requiring less than a month 'to learn to do well' fell more substantially, from 27% in 1986 to 20% in 2001.

Chart 4.1 Trends in qualifications used at work 1996-2001 (as %)

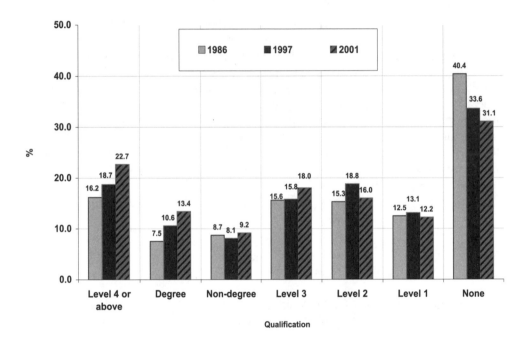

Note: 'Qualifications used' is based on data for qualifications required for the job, combined with estimates of the usefulness of qualifications once in the post.

Source: Alan Felstead, Duncan Gallie, Francis Green, *Work Skills in Britain 1986-2001*, DfES, 2002, p. 122.

The next 20 years

The demand for 'new economy' skills will grow. More people with 'knowledge' skills will work in existing occupations that have knowledge at their core, such as education and the professions. Openings for professionals are expected to grow by approaching 30% (867,000) in the current decade.[2]

[2] Institute for Employment Research, *Projections of Occupations and Qualifications 1999/2000*, Coventry and London: University of Warwick & DfEE, 2000.

Many workers will also be in new knowledge-intensive jobs, such as website designers, desktop publishers, biotechnology specialists, a variety of 'knowledge managers' who will help individuals manage the information glut, and the creative industries. The latter generated well over 100,000 jobs in London in the second half of the 1990s, behind 'business services' but substantially ahead of 'health and education', the third largest creator of jobs.[3]

The 'aesthetic economy' will become even more important. As low-cost manufactures flood the market from abroad, companies will make money not through making, but through designing and marketing. From movies to music to elegant mobile phones, profits will lie in 'hip and cool' – in products that appeal to the senses. Entertainment and consumption will continue to merge.

'Old economy' skills will remain important, too. The spread of knowledge-intensive work does not mean that the 'old economy' will wither away. The shift from manufacturing to services is sometimes equated with the demise of the twentieth century economy, but old economy jobs will still flourish.

They will be found in construction, which will be expected to meet the heavy demand for new homes projected over the next 20 years.[4] Millions of jobs will continue to exist in office, hotel and hospital cleaning, in security, in packaging and delivery, in driving lorries and taxis, in restaurants, cafes and bars, and in personal services.

These jobs will underpin the new economy. A media company for example needs to courier packages, have its post delivered, employ security personnel, have its offices cleaned, and have quality restaurants and other amenities nearby to attract high-calibre staff. 'Old economy' jobs will be the soil in which the 'new economy' will flourish.

Some of these jobs will be relatively unskilled, but a growing number will require intermediate and sometimes advanced skills. Waiters are beginning to use palm-held computers to transmit orders to the kitchen, for example, allowing them to serve the next customer more quickly and bills to be prepared automatically.

Even declining industries will have a substantial demand for skills. Openings due to people retiring, leaving through ill-health or moving to another job will exceed the number of job losses. For example, skilled jobs associated with metal and electrical industries are projected to contract by 408,000 between 2002 and 2012. But openings to replace existing workers will total 627,000, creating a net demand for skilled workers of 219,000.[5] The 'old economy' will require education and training as much as the new.

[3] Michael Moynagh & Richard Worsley, *Learning from the future: Scenarios for post-16 learning,* London: Learning and Skills Research Centre, 2003, p. 21.

[4] The Government expects the number of new households to increase from 21 to at least 24 million between 2001 and 2021, with possibly 190,000 new households forming each year. *Sustainable Communities: Homes for All. A Five Year Plan from the Office of the Deputy Prime Minister,* Cm 6424, London: The Stationery Office, 2005, p. 19.

[5] Institute for Employment Research, *Bulletin,* No. 73, 2004.

The demand for relationships skills will expand, as more jobs require high levels of 'emotional literacy' – the ability to respond helpfully to your own and other people's feelings, which is about more than just communication. The expansion of customer-facing jobs in which human interaction is central will help drive this

We noted in chapter 2 that as electronic intelligence continues to advance, it will take over many of the functions performed by knowledge workers.

"The obvious result of this long-term trend is a shift of value in jobs away from knowledge or skill, towards caring roles where workers are valued because they are people and their output is basically human interaction. Differentiators are then personality, warmth etc, rather than efficiency. We may call this the care economy."[6]

Emotional literacy will be vital in other occupations. As we have seen, human interactions are becoming more central to many jobs because of the need to pool knowledge by working collaboratively. Prominent among recent increases in generic skills have been communication and other human interactive skills, such as 'listening carefully to colleagues'.[7] 'Companies thrive on good company.'[8]

As the number of customer-focused jobs increases and technology advances, interpersonal skills will become even more important for organisational success. These skills will include not just written and oral communication, but personal presentation, dialogue skills, negotiating capacity, self-awareness, empathy and the ability to regulate one's own feelings.

Social capital – roughly defined as social relationships – is increasingly recognised as critical for organisational performance. Where social capital is high, it is argued, organisations can expect higher levels of trust and co operation, better knowledge sharing, greater coherence of action, lower turnover rates and more commitment.[9] But it remains a somewhat elusive concept, hard to pin down empirically. Techniques to measure and build social capital are still in their infancy.

A continuing need for 'life skills' will exist over and above work-related ones – anything from baking bread, growing your own vegetables, restoring a piece of furniture, parenting children to chairing meetings and organising events.

[6] Ian Pearson, "The future of the Care Economy", http://www.bt.com/innovation/viewpoints/pearson/care_economy.htm.
[7] Alan Felstead, Duncan Gallie, Francis Green, *op. cit.,* pp. 123-6.
[8] Quoted by Ken Starkey & Sue Tempest, 'Late Twentieth-Century Management, the Business School, and Social Capital' in Cary L. Cooper (ed.), *Leadership and Management in the 21st Century,* Oxford: OUP, 2005, p. 152.
[9] Ibid, pp 145-57.

These are skills that provide personal satisfaction and independence, and can empower individuals to add value to their communities. They can be seen as part of 'citizenship', as supporting the family, or as a means of building social capital and strengthening the voluntary sector. Life skills may have a growing 'market' especially among retired people, with more time to invest in them.

As the welfare state moves toward greater self-support, with government hoping that individuals will take more responsibility for their own pensions for example, life skills like debt management and the avoidance of mis-selling will be of growing importance. 'Liquid lives', involving more fluid life transitions and constant change at work, will require individuals to cope with new family arrangements and new job demands. The demand will grow for mentoring, coaching and parenting courses, for instance.

Community development will almost certainly remain a priority across the political spectrum, and this too may encourage help for people acquiring life skills. Policy-makers may also want to promote these skills among educationally disadvantaged people to increase their self-confidence and strengthen their position in the labour market.

Many of these skills will not be directly required at work, but they will provide support for a more competitive workplace. Acquiring them may increase individuals' self-confidence and enhance their generic skills, such as literacy or the ability to relate well to others. Individuals will have a stronger platform on which to build their employment skills.

What might be the implications?

Employers will upgrade their workers' skills as they move up the value chain and the demand for higher skills expands. In the 1970s employers were frequently blamed for not doing enough training. But then things began to change. Between 1986 and 1992 the proportion of employees reporting that they had received job-related training in the previous three years jumped from a third to more than a half. In this, Britain had become an international leader.[10] Global competition will continue to force organisations to devote more resources to training.

In particular, employers will invest heavily in coaching, mentoring and training courses to improve 'relationship' skills. This expenditure is likely to grow as consumers demand more of customer-facing staff, high-quality teamwork becomes even more vital and employers extend risk management to human resources – 'how can we cut the risk of absenteeism and turnover? Might better workplace relationships help?'

---

[10] Michael Moynagh & Richard Worsley, *op. cit.,* p. 38.

The expansion of employer-based training will probably hit supply bottlenecks. Already there are anecdotal complaints about the poor quality of much training – more training does not always mean better training. What new approaches will be developed in response?

Higher education will expand further, as part of the drive to a high-skill economy. Already China and India each produce around two million graduates a year, compared to about 250,000 in the UK. Over the next 20 years this will translate into a huge stock of skilled human capital abroad.[11] To prevent investment washing past Britain to these emerging economies, the government will seek both to increase the numbers going through higher education and to maintain its quality.

Government plans that by 2010 at least half of 18-30 year olds will have benefited from higher education, against the current 44%. The expansion is expected to come mainly through work-focused, two-year foundation degrees, but there seems little appetite for them at present. Instead, might students enrol for three years, but a growing number leave after two with a 'pass' rather than an 'honours' degree?

It is not unlikely that by the 2020s, two thirds of those under 30 – the current US rate – will enter higher education. The current increase in participation will generate the momentum for a further expansion.

As more people go to university, a degree will become the passport to a good job. Employers will assume that the pool of degree-holders now contains averagely able people and will refuse to consider non-graduates, except for low-paid jobs. Despite the costs, almost everyone will want a degree because almost everyone else has got one.

More people with degrees will force graduates to differentiate themselves, often by taking postgraduate qualifications. This will delay their entry into full-time jobs and further squeeze the labour supply. Yet governments will not stand in their way, partly to avoid frustrating young people's expectations, but also to help Britain keep ahead of the wave of graduates in Asia.

Key skills will become a higher priority in response to employer demands. Schools, colleges and universities will be under continuing pressure to deliver 'key' skills, on which individuals can later hang their job-specific skills. Current key skills include number, literacy, IT and communication. Some schools have added 'thinking' – the ability to construct and critique an argument. This may become a fifth key skill.

Embedding key skills into the schools' curriculum – and explicitly assessing them – is making slow headway. Most universities pay scant regard to key skills when selecting students. So schools and colleges catering for universities have little incentive to prioritise them, and this has influenced the attitude of the school sector as a whole.

---

[11] *Opportunity for all: The strength to take the long-term decisions for Britain. Pre-Budget Report,* cm 6408, London: The Stationery Office, 2004, p. 3.

Yet with the need to differentiate between a larger number of graduates, many with degrees at a similar level, might employers begin to recruit on the basis of key skills, using tests developed for this purpose? This would put pressure on the universities – and hence schools and colleges – to take key skills more seriously.

How to dig key skills into the curriculum will remain contentious. Some, as now, will argue that key skills can be included in the teaching of vocational subjects – literacy, IT, communication and thinking in the case of 'hotel management' for example – and be separately assessed.

Others will continue to maintain that key skills are best taught through traditional academic disciplines, and that too much emphasis on vocational subjects at a young age will disadvantage students in the workplace. 'Practical' subjects may impede the learning of number, literacy and thinking skills, for example, which will be essential foundations for the life-long learning many workers will require. Might targeting vocational courses at academic low-achievers deprive them of the very skills they need?[12]

The key skill of 'communication' may be extended to 'emotional literacy'. Already some schools, to avoid excluding pupils, are teaching emotional literacy to improve standards of behaviour and discipline.

This trend may accelerate as employers become more aware of the vital contribution of social capital to competitiveness. With collaboration at the heart of many jobs and the customer interface of growing importance, employers will give preference to applicants who can demonstrate competence in interpersonal skills. As social capital is recognised as central to organisational success – as important as IT and other skills – the education system will be forced to respond.

Recognising emotional literacy as a key skill would require something of a revolution in the education system. In its 2004 five-year strategy for education, the Government listed the skills young people will need as they enter the workforce. There was no explicit mention of the broad range of interpersonal skills. The closest reference was to the need for communication skills. But as illustrated by the example given in the strategy ('writing well'), this is not the same.[13]

A greater emphasis on 'social capital' skills would raise questions about the trend toward individualised pedagogies. Can personalised learning and teaching be combined with group-based approaches? Will new methodologies be developed to define, teach, measure and assess emotional literacy from a young age?

---

[12] Alison Wolf, *Does Education Matter?* London: Penguin, 2002, pp. 93-7.
[13] Department for Education and Skills, *Five-Year Strategy for Children and Learners,* Cm 6272, London: Stationery Office, 2004, ch. 6, para. 20.

Points to take away

• The demand for knowledge skills will include those in the so-called 'aesthetic economy', alongside a continuing demand for more traditional skills.

• The demand for interpersonal skills will be especially important, and has yet to be fully reflected in educational strategy.

Who will do this work?

5. More older workers?

• The employment rate for 50 to 64 year olds has risen gradually since the mid 1990s. The rate for people who have reached the state pension age has also begun to creep up.

• Significantly more older workers below the state pension age will remain in employment, but for much of the next 20 years employment will increase only slowly among workers above the pension age.

• The growing number of 50 to 64 year olds with jobs will clear the ground for more people to work beyond 65 in the longer term. Employers need to prepare now for more older workers.

Not many days pass without some media story about Britain's ageing population. The UK faces a growing demand for labour on one hand and, like other more developed countries, needs to support a 'greying' population on the other. Unsurprisingly, many commentators suggest that older workers will square the circle. Older people will stay in employment for longer, giving them more time to build up a pension and boosting the tax-take.

To support an ageing society, the government has declared an aspiration for 80% of the working-age population to be in employment – up from almost 75% today. This relies heavily on encouraging older workers below the state pension age to keep working. In addition, the government wants to increase the employment of people above the state pension age.[1]

A longer working life would mean that more people would be in employment to support those who had retired. It would also help to meet the growing demand for labour discussed in chapter 2. But up to what age will older people be willing to stay in work?

The story so far

The employment rate for older men fell substantially between 1950 and 1995. In the 1950s and 60s this was due mostly to a fall in the proportion of men aged 65 to 69 in employment – from 48% in 1952 to 30% in 1971, very high figures compared with today.[2] The decline continued, so that by the 1990s only seven to eight per cent of men who had reached the state pension age were employed.[3]

---

[1] *Department for Work and Pensions Five Year Strategy. Opportunity and security throughout life,* cm 6447, London: the Stationery Office, 2005, pp. 25-6.

[2] *Pensions: Challenges and Choices. The First Report of the Pensions Commission,* London: The Stationery Office, 2004, p. 34.

[3] ONS Labour Market Statistics – Integrated FR LFS TIME PERIODS, Table YBUQ.

Between the mid 1970s and mid 90s a second trend developed. The proportion of 50 to 64 year old men with jobs fell sharply – from 88% in 1973 to 63% in 1995. The falls bunched around the two recessions in the early 1980s and early 90s, when a large number of manufacturing jobs in particular were lost. Employment rates for women held up (see Chart 5.1).

Chart 5.1 Employment Rates for Men and Women aged 50 - SPA: 1973-1995

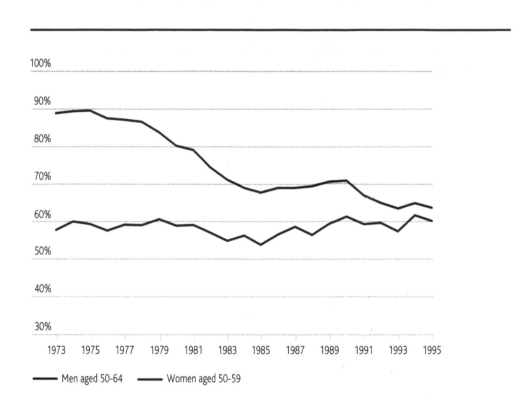

Source: *Pensions: Challenges and Choices. The First Report of the Pensions Commission,* London: The Stationery Office, 2004, Figure 2.9.

Employment rates for men and women aged 50 to state pension age have risen gradually since the mid 1990s, reversing the decline in male employment (see Chart 5.2). This has reflected the tightening of the labour market, government efforts to encourage people off incapacity-related benefits and the squeeze on direct contribution pensions: stock market declines since 2000 cut the value of individual pension funds, while the post-1998 fall in annuity rates sliced the size of pension those funds could buy.[4]

---

[4] *Pensions: Challenges and Choices. op. cit.,* p. 38.

Chart 5.2 Employment Rates for Men and Women aged 50 - SPA: 1993-2004

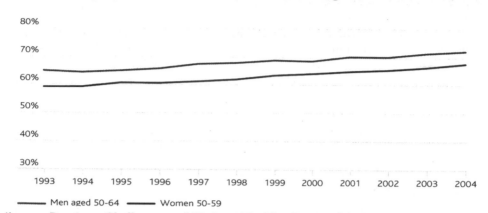

Source: *Pensions: Challenges and Choices.* The First Report of the Pensions Commission, London: The Stationery Office, 2004, Figure 2:12.

Employment rates for men and women who have reached state pension age have also started to creep up. (see Chart 5.3) This has been most marked for women, for whom the rate has moved from 7.83% in 1998 to 9.85% in 2004. For men the trend has been more gradual, from 7.30% in 2001 to 8.55%. Working beyond the state pension age is just beginning to spread, but has yet to take off.

Older workers are more likely to be self-employed, to work part-time and to have fewer qualifications than 25 to 49 year olds.[5]

Chart 5.3 Employment rates for men and women of state pension age and above (UK, %, men, 65+, %, women, 60+)

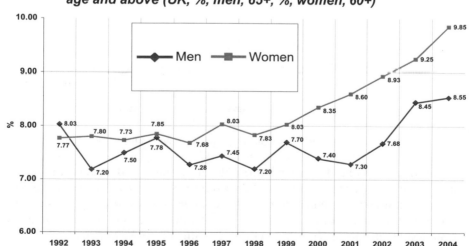

Source: ONS Labour Market Statistics – Integrated FR LFS TIME PERIODS, Tables YBUQ, YBUR.

---

[5] *Welfare to Work: Tackling the Barriers to the Employment of Older People, Report by the Comptroller and Auditor General,* London: The Stationery Office, 2004, p. 20.

The next 20 years

Over the next two decades, employment rates among older men and women below state pension age will continue to rise significantly, but for much of the period they will increase more slowly among workers above the pension age. Several factors will lie behind this 'up till I retire, but not much beyond' story.

First, the supply of younger workers will tighten. Over the period as a whole there will be a strong demand for labour, as we have seen. At the same time, a shrinking pool of young full-time workers will constrain the supply.

This will not be due to a demographic fall in the total number of young people, as is often supposed. The big drop has already occurred – in the case of the twenties age group, from about 9.1 million in 1991 to almost 7.5 million in 2001. The number of 20 to 29 year olds will actually increase by 2011, before tailing away gradually thereafter. In 2026, the number in this age group is projected to be only fractionally less than in 2011 (see Chart 5.4).

Chart 5.4 *Estimated number of young people in the UK*

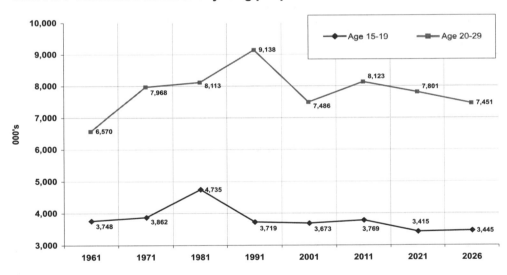

Source: *Annual Abstract of Statistics,* London: The Stationery Office, 2004, p. 28.

More important will be the extension of education, largely driven by the need to create a 'high skills' economy that can beat off threats from low-skilled competitors abroad. The numbers in sixth forms and FE colleges are set to increase[6] – and this will fuel the expansion of universities. Historically, as more 16 to 19 year olds have stayed in education, the numbers going to university have risen.[7]

---

[6] The government intends that everyone will have the opportunity to stay in school, college or work-related training till the age of 19. *Britain forward not back: The Labour Party manifesto 2005,* pp. 39-40.

[7] Alison Wolf, *Does Education Matter?* London: Penguin, 2002, p. 174.

Current plans to expand higher education will generate further growth, because as more people enter university others will be forced to go too: a degree will be vital to get an 'average' job. Employers wanting to fill ordinary jobs will turn down their noses at people without degrees since the enlarged pool of graduates will now contain averagely-able people. By the 2020s, two thirds of school-leavers under 30 may enter higher education, against just over two-fifths today.[8]

All this will take a growing proportion of young people out of full-time employment. A report from City and Guilds suggests that 16 to 25 year olds will comprise just 11% of the workforce in 2020, compared to 16% today – a plunge of nearly one million.[9]

Many students of course will work part-time to keep down their student loans, which will offset some of the drop in young people's full-time employment. Other offsetting factors may be immigration and the employment of more adults in the prime of life, discussed in the next two chapters. Yet even allowing for these possibilities, it is hard to see how today's skill shortages will be reversed, especially when the economy is growing. Many employers will be under pressure to keep their older workers.

Secondly, more people aged 50 to 64 will stay in employment. This will come about partly for demographic reasons – the number of 50 to 64 year olds in the population will go up (see Chart 5.5).

Chart 5.5 UK population of 50 to 65 year olds, estimates & projections

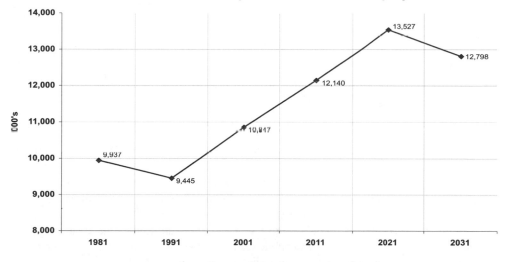

Source: "Government Actuary's population projections", 10 March, 2003. http:/www.gad. gov.uk/Population/2003/uk/wuk03singyear.xls.

Note: 1991 and 2001 figures not revised in light of 2001 census.

---

[8] See chapter 4.
[9] 'Young people set to become a rare breed in the UK workplace', City & Guilds of London Institute press release, 23 May 2005.

The state pension age for women is due to be equalised with men in stages between 2010 and 2020, which will encourage more women to work till they are 65. A growing number of men will also keep working till their mid-60s to secure an adequate retirement income – they will not have the redundancy payouts that encouraged early retirement in the 1980s and early 90s.

Public sector pension schemes with 'retirement' ages below the private sector will gradually bring their ages into line with private schemes, to ease the burden on public finances. This will encourage public sector workers to stay longer in their jobs. Government initiatives to help disabled people stay in employment or return to work could increase the employment rate of older people, too.[10]

But thirdly, the 'lucky generation' now approaching retirement will have weak incentives to work beyond the state pension age. By and large, newly retired households will be financially better off than previous generations. More women workers, who will be entitled to a pension in their own right, will be retiring between now and 2025. Raising their state pension age will give them more time to save for retirement, boosting the household incomes of couples reaching the pension age.

A sizeable majority of those retiring in the next 20 years will have a second pension.[11] Despite the waning membership of occupational schemes since the 1970s, many retirees will still enjoy relatively generous final salary pensions.[12] It will be the under 45s, coming up behind, who will have to rely on less generous DC schemes and work till they are older to make up the difference.[13]

Those approaching retirement will also be rather more likely than their predecessors to have inherited significant sums from their home-owning parents, and to own their own home outright by age 65.[14] To finance their old age, will home-owners increasingly downsize (with growing numbers moving abroad) or use equity release to supplement their retirement incomes?

---

[10] *Department for Work and Pensions Five Year Strategy.* op. cit., pp. 40-51. These initiatives are discussed in ch. 7 below.

[11] Around 60% of the *population* aged 20 to 65 has a 'second tier' pension, which is compulsory for all employees (but not the self-employed). *Pensions: Challenges and Choices. The First Report of the Pensions Commission,* op. cit., pp. 70-1.

[12] In 2000 there were about 4.6 million active members of private sector defined benefit schemes and about the same number in public sector schemes. *Pensions: Challenges and Choices. The First Report of the Pensions Commission,* op. cit., p. 84.

[13] Whereas 26% of all private sector employees belonged to salary related schemes in 2003, just 14% of new employees were in these schemes, down from 19% in 1998. *Pensions: Challenges and Choices. The First Report of the Pensions Commission,* op. cit., pp. 83-4.

[14] Michael Moynagh & Richard Worsley, *The Opportunity of a Lifetime: Reshaping Retirement,* London: CIPD, 2004, pp. 105-9. For example, in 2000 74% of 60 to 64 year olds owned their own home, 75% of 55 to 59 year olds did so and 77% of 50 to 54 year olds. Just 22% of 60 to 64 year olds were still repaying a mortgage.

Fourthly, barriers to working beyond 65 could persist for some time, despite a continuing drive to end age discrimination at work. Government has announced that before the end of 2006, as part of legislation to implement the European Directive on age discrimination, it will outlaw mandatory retirement before the age of 65, unless it can be justified. Employees above that age will be entitled to request to remain in employment, which employers will have a duty to consider. This provision in the legislation will be reviewed in 2011.

Pressure to go further and totally abolish mandatory retirement will grow. Steadily more people live 'liquid lives' in which transitions are individualised. The idea that there is a 'right time' to move from one phase of life to the next is being replaced by the motto, 'it's up to you'. Transitions are based on choice rather than age – and this is especially true for the better-educated and better-off. The notion that there is a set time when 'you have to retire' will seem increasingly quaint.

The baby boom generation will enter their sixties over the next two decades. This age group has spent its life fighting various forms of discrimination based on gender, race, disability and sexual orientation. So its mindset will be sympathetic to complaints about age discrimination at work. The number of baby boomers will give these complaints considerable force. Almost certainly, demands to scrap all forms of mandatory retirement will become irresistible – if not in 2011, then soon after.

But what will be the effect of abolishing mandatory retirement? Much will depend on how attractive employers make it to stay on. Many workers feel too 'worn and torn' to continue in full-time jobs beyond their mid 60s. Almost two-fifths of people aged 65 to 74 report having a long-standing illness that limits their activities.[15] If global competition intensifies the pressures at work, employees may feel even less inclined to remain beyond retirement age.

Part-time work, downsizing and other means of phasing the transition from work to retirement could make continued employment attractive. But many employers, who are often inherently cautious, may be reluctant to take these initiatives.

Squeezed by costs, they may wince at the overhead expense of flexible work – the same payroll costs for a part-timer as a full-timer, for instance, or the management time required for new approaches. Allowing older people to work more flexibly might spark similar requests from younger workers with children. Far from improving, skill shortages might get worse as younger employees go part-time.

So although legal restraints on working beyond the retirement age will almost certainly be relaxed during the next decade, realistic openings could well remain limited.

---

[15] Alison O'Connell, *Raising State Pension Age: Are We Ready?*, London: Pensions Policy Institute, 2002, p. 24.

What might be the implications?

The number of 50 to 64 year olds in employment will continue to rise, due to tight labour markets and a growing supply of older people who want to stay in work. Might the proportion be approaching 80% by the early 2020s, eight per cent higher than today – not totally unrealistic given that 88% of men in the age group were employed in 1973?

On the other hand, relatively generous pensions (plus other sources of income) and limited employment opportunities will keep the number working beyond the state pension age to a trickle over the next few years. This trickle may expand to a stream once mandatory retirement is abolished, but it is unlikely to become a river till those behind the 'lucky generation', with less generous pensions, reach their mid 60s after 2025. The Future Foundation anticipates that 13% (1.8 million people) will be working beyond the state pension age in 2020, compared with about 9% today.[16]

In 2004 nearly 70% of 50 to 64 year olds were in employment, against slightly under 80% for 25 to 34 year olds and just over 82% for the 35 to 49 age group. Had the participation rate for 50 to 64 year olds been five per cent higher in 2004, not implausible over the next two decades, an extra 451,000 people would have been in employment – a significant boost to the labour supply.[17]

This increase will help prepare the ground for more people to work beyond 65 in due course. A growing number of workers in their early to mid 60s would erode the age discrimination that still persists in the workplace[18] – 'if they can handle the job now, why not in two years' time?' As the total working beyond 65 expands slowly, more people will see that delaying retirement is a viable option.[19]

A long-term pension settlement is not unlikely in the years ahead. It could well involve:

> • greater encouragement to save for a pension, perhaps by deeming employees to have contracted into an occupational scheme offered by their employer;

---

[16] '63% increase in the number of people working past statutory retirement age by 2020', Saga Press Release, 25 September 2003. The full report, prepared by the Future Foundation for Saga, is not available.

[17] The Turner Report suggested a 'stretching but feasible' scenario whereby the employment rate for 50 to 64 year old men rose by around 7% by 2050, and for women by 16% (*Pensions: Challenges and Choices. The First Report of the Pensions Commission,* op. cit., p. 40).

[18] For example, a 2003 survey of working and retired people found that one-fifth of respondents claimed to have been discouraged from applying for a job because an advert 'contained or hinted at an age range'. 35% claimed to have been discriminated against at work on grounds of age, far higher than any other category (such as race, gender or disability). *Age, pensions and retirement: Attitudes and expectations,* London: CIPD, 2003, Tables 5 & 14.

[19] Only 17% of men aged 67, for example, were in employment in 2004. *Challenges and Choices. The First Report of the Pensions Commission,* op. cit., p. 42.

> • a higher basic state pension to reduce means testing;
>
> • later retirement to help pay for this, perhaps by increasing the state pension most sharply for those who work beyond 65;
>
> • pressure on employers to introduce phased retirement, so that staying in work beyond 65 becomes more attractive.

As the pension 'time bomb' approaches, achieving this settlement will become politically more urgent.[20] Higher levels of employment among workers approaching retirement may come to be seen as a vital first step.

Making employment attractive to older workers will become urgent. This will not be just a matter of good HR practice: in the face of tight labour markets, it will be a commercial priority. Senior managers who have ignored the issue could be in trouble with their Boards – 'why didn't you warn us about skill shortages?'

Tackling the challenge then may be too late. Changing policy and practice can take a long time. The effects of early retirement in the 1980s and early 90s were felt for many years – in the scarcity of employees aged 50-plus, for example. Attracting workers in their mid sixties will require new approaches to performance appraisals and flexi-time. These cannot be introduced overnight. Employers may need a five-year strategy, perhaps longer.

Organisations wanting to be ahead of the game will need to start early. They may have to work with their pension trustees to change the rules of their occupational schemes. They may need to overcome trade union fears that cooperation would legitimise 'work till you drop' employment – cooperation may have to be based on an agenda of employee choice.

Might employers who get everyone on side now be able to say one day, 'We've been developing policies to employ older workers for some time, and have stolen a march on our competitors'?

More older workers will be accompanied by fewer younger workers, as we have seen. Even now, according to City and Guilds, over half of British companies have experienced recent difficulty in recruiting young, skilled staff.[21] These difficulties will persist as more young people remain in education, shrinking the pool of 16 to 25 year olds available for full-time work.

Employers may need to rethink radically their retention and recruitment strategies, focusing on the empowerment of, and respect for young people. They may need to develop innovative graduate apprenticeship schemes, involving for example a pre-university 'gap' year of paid on-the-job training, employment during the vacations and a final apprenticeship year after graduation. Remuneration packages may need to include housing support.

---

[20] The pressures to achieve this are well set out in *Pensions: Challenges and Choices. The First Report of the Pensions Commission,* op. cit.

[21] 'Young people set to become a rare breed in the UK workplace', City & Guilds of London Institute press release, 23 May 2005.

Points to take away

• Over the next 20 years we can expect more 50 to 64 year olds in employment, but the number of workers aged 65-plus will creep up slowly.

• Attracting older workers will become increasingly urgent for organisations, preparing for this will take time and employers would be well advised to start their preparations now.

6. More workers from abroad?

• Only recently has immigration exceeded emigration from Britain. The majority of immigrants are dependents rather than workers.

• The demand for migrant labour will continue to rise, as will the potential supply. Interests favouring and opposed to immigration will be finely balanced.

• Even high numbers of migrant workers will not be a labour market panacea. Migration will increase the diversity of British society, strengthen the informal economy and bring mixed benefits to countries of origin.

Immigration is a highly charged topic. Many fear that Britain is being swamped by arrivals from overseas. Others recognise that skill shortages are a problem, boosting the labour supply is therefore urgent and controlled immigration would help. How might this debate play out over the next 20 years?

The story so far

The international migration tradition in Britain is one of net emigration rather than immigration. This was true even in the 1950s and 60s, when successive waves of immigrants came first from the Caribbean, then India and then Bangladesh, with their dependents continuing to arrive thereafter.[1] Throughout the period, these arrivals were offset by substantial emigration.

It is only since the early 1980s that (in most years[2]) Britain has become a net importer of people.[3] Chart 6.1 shows how net migration into the UK has increased substantially since the late 1990s. Net inflows reached 172,000 in 2001, falling away to 153,000 in 2002. Over the decade to 2002, approaching 3.9 million people entered the country as migrants and 2.8 million left, giving a net inflow of over one million.

---

[1] By 1971 primary immigration from the New Commonwealth had largely come to an end, due to the progressive tightening of restrictions on entry. Stephen Glover et al, *Migration: an economic and social analysis,* RDS Occasional Paper No. 67, London: Home Office, 2001, p. 7.
[2] 1988, 1992 and 1993 were exceptions. Stephen Glover et al, *op. cit.,* p. 9.
[3] David Coleman, 'Demographic, economic and social consequences of UK migration' in Helen Disney (ed.), *Work in Progress. Migration, Integration and the European Labour Market,* London: Civitas, 2003, p. 9.

Chart 6.1 Total International Migration, UK (000s, to nearest 000)

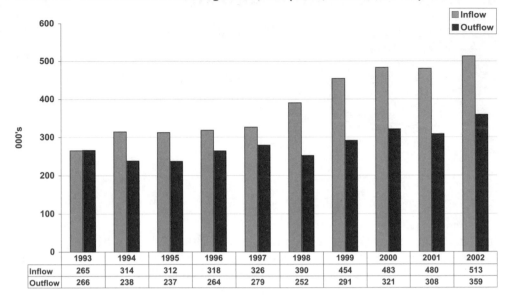

	1993	1994	1995	1996	1997	1998	1999	2000	2001	2002
Inflow	265	314	312	318	326	390	454	483	480	513
Outflow	266	238	237	264	279	252	291	321	308	359

Source: ONS, International Migration 2002 Series MN No. 29, Table 2.9.

Immigration does not equal extra labour, although 'passengers given leave to enter the UK in employment-related categories' increased from around 105,000 in 1995 to 180,000 in 2003.[4] However, it is worth emphasising that a substantial number of arrivals were not workers.

The pressure group, Migration Watch UK, has estimated the composition of migrants over the five years 1998-2002, based on grants of settlement (see Table 6A). The high proportion of dependents ('family formation') stands out. In fact, the overall figure for dependents is considerably higher because 'Employment' and 'Asylum' included dependents, who in the case of 'Employment' were about half the total.[5] Most of these dependents were not looking for jobs.[6]

---

[4] *Controlling our borders: Making migration work for Britain. Five year strategy for asylum and immigration,* cm 6472, London: The Stationery Office, 2005, p. 14.

[5] It should be noted that 'Employment' figures are in respect of Work Permits issued four years earlier, and so do not reflect fully the high inflows since the late 1990s.

[6] Migration Watch UK has been the centre of controversy because of its calls to stem the inflow of migrants and its projections for future inflows, which are higher than the Government's. However, its figures are based on scholarly work, including that by the respected Oxford demographer, Dr David Coleman.

Table 6A: Composition of grants of settlement, 1998-2002

Category	
Employment	14%
Asylum	30%
Family formation	48%
Discretionary grants	8%
Category unknown	<1%

Source: 'How skilled are immigrants to Britain?', http://www.migrationwatchuk.org/Briefingpapers/other/howskilledareimmigrantstobritain.asp (accessed 14/07/04).

The skills profile of employed immigrants is polarised. Many are highly skilled, such as the estimated 150,000-plus French entrepreneurs who moved to the UK in 1995-2000, attracted in part by lower taxes and the Channel Tunnel transport link.[7] Most of the work permits issued in 2002-3 were for skilled workers. Twenty-three per cent of them (almost 29,000) were issued to nurses. Teachers numbered 8000. Chefs accounted for 5000.

A minority were for less-skilled workers - in hotel/catering for instance (nearly 2000).[8] To these must be added foreign students working part-time or temporarily in unskilled jobs, seasonal workers in agriculture and those working without any kind of permit in construction.

The next 20 years

The demand for migrant labour will continue to rise in the more developed countries, partly because of the growing need for skills. 'Just look at Silicon Valley's large supply of successful Indian and Taiwanese computer scientists and venture capitalists. The enhanced appetite for such professionals reflects the shift to a globalised economy in which countries compete for markets by creating and attracting technically skilled talent.'[9]

Acute skill shortages are forecast for health, education and other sectors in the UK. For example, based on the number of graduates in the late 1990s, schools and colleges would need to recruit a massive 12% of the graduate population a year over the next decade merely to replace the large number of teachers who are due to retire. The Teacher Training Agency has attempted to recruit on to PGCE courses a fifth of all geography and music graduates, over a third of maths graduates and 43% of all linguists.[10]

---

[7] Stephen Glover et al, op. cit., p. 32.

[8] 'How skilled are immigrants to Britain', http://www.migrationwatchuk.org/Briefingpapers/other/howskilledareimmigrantstobritain.asp (accessed 14/07/04).

[9] Jagdish Bhagwati, *In Defense of Globalisation,* New York: OUP, 2004, p. 213.

[10] Matthew Horne, *Classroom assistance. Why teachers must transform teaching,* London: Demos, 2002, pp. 13-4.

At the same time, the demand will grow for workers in lower-skilled jobs. Not least, greater prosperity will allow more people to pay for child and elder-care. In 1996 over half the legal immigrants to the USA were women, their median age was 29 and many were employed in care work, such as Filipino women caring for the children of American professionals.[11] Shortages of care workers are already acute in the UK and are set to grow (see chapter 17).

British universities will increase their intake of foreign students as the higher education market becomes more international. The UK has a number of universities that are well placed to compete globally. Experience suggests that a significant proportion of overseas students will seek employment in Britain. An estimated 70% of foreign-born PhD graduates remain in the United States, many becoming citizens.[12]

The supply of migrant labour will grow, too. The UN projects the expansion of international migration (workers and dependents) from today's estimated 175 million to 250 million by 2050. This would be roughly in step with world population growth.

The projection is almost certainly too cautious. It would represent a much slower rate of growth than in the recent past – an increase of 43% over the next 50 years compared to 133% over the last 40. Historically, there is plenty of room for expansion. Around 3% of the world's population currently live outside their country of birth, against an estimated 10% who migrated between 1870 and 2025.[13] Migration is driven not by overall population growth, but by economic and political factors – especially economic.

Better education in the emerging economies will be one such factor. Fifty-two per ·cent of boys and 33% of girls in South Asia are now in high school, and both figures will increase.[14] Higher education will also continue to expand. As education widens individuals' horizons and increases their confidence, more people may be ready to work abroad. Higher skills will equip them for many of the jobs on offer.

Education can also act as a bridge between cultures, giving workers from less developed countries the cultural skills to undertake care and other relatively unskilled jobs in more developed ones. An American study found that over half the migrant nannies interviewed had college degrees.[15]

---

[11] Arlie Russell Hochschild, 'Global Care Chains and Emotional Surplus Value' in Will Hutton & Anthony Giddens (eds), *On The Edge,* London: Vintage, 2001, pp. 130-46.

[12] Jagdish Bhagwati, *op. cit.,* p. 214.

[13] HM Treasury, *Long-term global economic challenges and opportunities for the UK,* London: The Stationery Office, 2004, p. 25.

[14] Jerome C. Glenn & Theodore J. Gordon, *2004 State of the Future*, Washington: American Council for the United Nations University, 2004, p. 33.

[15] Arlie Russell Hochschild, *op. cit.,* p 138.

Global wage inequalities will provide an incentive for teachers, nurses and other skilled workers to seek employment abroad – at least for a time – at higher-wages.[16] Remittances from foreign-born workers to their families at home are substantial. In 1993 officially recorded remittances were worth 44% of Bangladesh's exports and 24% of Pakistan's; in 1990 they accounted for 13% of India's. Remittances through informal channels – such as cash sent with friends or relatives, or gifts of clothes and other consumer goods – probably double or even triple the recorded amount.[17]

The potential is vast. Indian-born residents in the United States account for just 0.1% of the American population, but their aggregate income is worth 10% of India's GDP.[18] As more people work abroad permanently or temporarily, others will see the advantages and want to follow suit.

Moving to a new country will be easier, as the world continues to get better connected. Despite higher energy prices, travel costs in real terms may well continue to fall because of technology-induced greater fuel efficiency. The financial ability to undertake the journey is a big constraint on emigration.

Improved telecommunications will provide quicker, fuller and more accurate information about potential jobs and travel alternatives, reducing dependence on less reliable, informal networks. By the end of the decade, 50% of all internet users could live in the developing world, against a mere 4% in 2003.[19]

A more open world will mean that people will travel more and have greater awareness of opportunities around the globe. International journeys are projected to more than double between 2002 and 2020, from 703 million to 1.6 billion a year.[20] More than 50% of illegal immigrants to the US first arrive as tourists.[21]

---

[16] The global pay gap may be especially marked for professional and other highly skilled jobs. Professional salaries in poor countries will tend to be depressed by low levels of pay generally, which will limit what these countries can afford. Rich countries, on the other hand, will afford higher salaries as top earnings continue to accelerate at a rapid rate.

[17] Shivani Puri & Tineke Ritzema, *Migrant Worker Remittances, Micro-finance and the Informal Economy: Prospects and Issues,* International Labour Organisation, Social Finance Unit, Working Paper No. 21, last updated 1999, http://www.ilo.org/public/english/ employment/finance/papers/wpap21.htm.

[18] Jagdish Bhagwati, *op. cit.,* p 215.

[19] HM Treasury, *Long-term global economic challenges and opportunities for the UK,* London: The Stationery Office, 2004, p. 30.

[20] World Tourism Organisation, *Tourism 2020 Vision,* www. world-tourism.org/market_ research/facts/ menu.html.

[21] Jagdish Bhagwati, *op. cit.,* pp. 214-6.

The expansion of the EU has made it easier for many Eastern Europeans to seek work in Britain. Between 1 May 2004 when eight countries formally joined the union and the end of the year, around 130,000 people from the new member states registered for work in the UK.[22]

The accession of these and perhaps – over the next 20 years – other comparatively low-wage countries could transform the ethnic balance of new arrivals (though the numbers from Eastern Europe should tail off as living standards in those countries rise). Might immigration become more of a 'white' phenomenon?

Migration will be self-reinforcing. When immigrants settle, they form communities that welcome further arrivals from their part of the world, help newcomers make a home and put them in touch with useful networks. The more immigration, the larger these communities will be and the wider their networks.

Increased migration will strengthen the vested interests in favour of immigration. The electoral influence of immigrant communities will grow, and they will be supported by civil rights and other pressure groups. Governments will find it difficult to curb the arrival of dependents.

As more employers rely on foreign-born workers rather than adopt alternative methods of production, the economic case for migration will strengthen. Even now, the hospitality industry argues that many firms would not survive without temporary migrant labour, with dire consequences for Britain's tourist industry.

Interests favouring and opposed to immigration will be finely balanced. Many employers will support a liberal approach to migrant workers. They will range from farmers, meat-packers, restauranteurs and others who rely on cheap overseas labour to banks, hospitals and universities who need skilled immigrants for specialised jobs.

Supporting them will be the Treasury, which needs immigration to keep the population expanding. Officials estimate that current levels of immigration add almost 0.5% to economic growth. Chopping away that half percentage point would seriously dent tax receipts. Alongside the Treasury will be the Bank of England, which will welcome foreign workers when labour markets are tight. Immigration will dampen wage pressures, taking the heat off interest rates.[23]

Joining these economic interests will be affluent middle classes and young professionals, who will be sympathetic to immigration on grounds of fairness and the attractions of an ethnically mixed society. They will include parents employing child minders from abroad, people with ageing relatives who rely on migrant carers, and all those who enjoy leisure and other facilities employing foreign workers.

---

[22] 'Worker Registration Scheme and Work Permit Figures Published', Home Office Press Release, 22 Feb. 2005.
[23] Anatole Kaletsky, 'Political flaw at the heart of Tory view of "damage" done by migrants', *The Times,* 26 April 2005.

Against this formidable coalition will be lower-paid workers who fear immigrants will take their jobs or lower their wages. With them will be people who fear loss of national identity ('are we being swamped?'), loss of control over UK borders and health tourism.

Allied to them will be parts of government that are concerned about transport congestion and housing shortages, and residents in the South East who fear overcrowding. Immigration is a major driver of housing demand, for example. One estimate, based on official statistics, suggests that a third of the projected demand for extra housing between 1996 and 2021 will be due to immigration.[24] Most immigrants come to London and the South East, where overcrowding is thought to be especially acute.

To manage these anxieties, the Government proposes to introduce a transparent points system for all who come to work in the UK, allow only skilled workers to settle long-term, end the immediate or automatic right of relatives to bring in more relatives, take further action to prevent abuse of the asylum system and further strengthen border controls.[25]

The aim is to increase public confidence in the system. If fears of being over-run can be allayed and clear skills-based criteria for immigration be established, it is hoped that there will be greater support for immigration to meet Britain's labour market needs.

This approach could have some success. At 8,465, asylum applications in the final quarter of 2004 were 22% lower than in the equivalent period the year before, and 68% lower than the peak in October 2002. They were at their second lowest level since 1997. Four out of five claims were decided in two months compared to the 20 months it took in 1997.[26] Government clearly has the ability to gain greater control over immigration – and in time ID cards may provide a new means of stopping illegal entrants.

But will reducing the number of asylum seekers and illegal immigrants be enough? Might public concern then shift to economic migrants, or will the need for imported skills outweigh these concerns? Distasteful though the thought is, might a partial shift to white, European migration help to make immigration more acceptable, or will colour prove irrelevant because concerns are focused on overcrowding?

---

[24] Based on the Government's 2000 housing projections (which included a sensitivity analysis of the effects of additional net migration) and the Government Actuary's Department 2004 revised population projections, 4.53 million new homes will be required over this period, of which 1.46 million will be due to immigration. 'Housing and immigration - an update', www. migrationwatchuk.org/frameset.asp?menu=publications&page=publications.asp. (accessed 2/12/04).

[25] *Controlling our borders*, op. cit.,

[26] 'Asylum Applications Continue to Fall', Home Office Press Release, 22 Feb. 2005.

What might be the implications?

Three projections for net immigration for the period 2003 to 2031 have been prepared by the Government Actuary's Department.[27]

- The 'principal projection' (which is used in its population projections) assumes that net inward migration to the UK averages 130,000 a year.

- The 'high migration variant' assumes that net inward migration averages 190,000.

- The 'low migration variant' puts the figure at 70,000.

Though many of these immigrants will not be employed, might tight labour markets keep net migration at higher levels than the 'principal projection' of 130,000 a year, at least for a while? Recorded net migration averaged 158,000 in the five years before 2004. Reducing the number of asylum seekers would bring the figure down, but encouraging economic migration would push it up.[28]

Immigration will not be a labour market panacea, though migrant workers will certainly bring economic benefits and ease skill shortages in the short term. One reason for the dynamism of London's economy is the large number of foreign-born workers. Government estimates that net inward migration will contribute 10-15% of the trend economic growth forecast for the UK.[29]

However, new arrivals will not automatically boost the labour supply. Many will be non-working dependents, who along with migrant workers will raise overall demand in the economy, particularly for housing. This in turn will increase the demand for labour, offsetting some of the supply-side benefits of migration.

Nor will immigration be a long-term solution to our ageing society. In the short term, a net increase in younger overseas workers will boost the numbers in employment who support the older population. But in the long run, immigration will be unable to preserve the current ratio of workers to dependents.

As today's immigrants age, together with others in the population, even more immigrants would be needed to maintain the support ratio. As they in turn age, the number of immigrants would have to rise still further. One estimate suggests that using immigration to preserve the current support ratio would raise the UK

---

[27] 'Migration and population growth', http://www.gad.gov.uk/Population/2003/methodology/ mignote.htm (accessed 2/12/04)

[28] Migration Watch UK, 'Government Actuary's Department 2003-based population projections', http://www.migrationwatchuk.org/frameset.asp?menu=faqs&page=whatsnew.asp (accessed 1/3/05).

[29] *Controlling our borders,* op. cit., p. 11.

population from around 60 million to 120 million by 2050 and to 312 million by 2100, not much less than the 2003 population of the whole EU![30]

The only thing that would change this would be a large number of older Britons retiring abroad. Younger arrivals would be offset by older people leaving the country. There is certainly a trend in this direction. 42% of real estate buyers in Spain are British. 500,000 Britons own a home in Spain, with half of them living there for six months or more a year.[31]

Higher UK property prices than on the continent could encourage people retiring to trade down by moving abroad, accelerating the trend. Is it significant that Thomson's travel agency opening an estate agency arm for people who want to buy properties in Europe? This is a trend well worth watching. It could easily be one of tomorrow's big surprises, and upset many of today's demographic projections.

If this trend does not take off, however, persuading older workers to stay in employment, perhaps by increasing the incentives to do so, will be a more effective long-term solution to the ageing population and labour shortages than immigration. Will fewer migrants and more older workers eventually become higher government priorities?

Migration will increase the diversity of British society by swelling the size of ethnic communities already here. Workplaces will become more ethnically mixed, which will keep diversity high on employers' agendas. Racism is still extensive in many organisations, despite management and union efforts to stamp it out.[32]

Migration will also widen cleavages within ethnic communities. Already differences exist between recent arrivals from traditional backgrounds, and second and third generations who are adopting values more widespread in Britain. Newcomers from strong faith and traditional backgrounds will reinforce these differences. Traditional forms of Christianity, Islam and other faiths will get a boost, just as many British-born blacks and members of other ethnic minorities will be adapting their traditions to the surrounding culture.

Census data indicates that in most cases, minority ethnic groups have become slightly less geographically concentrated. Indian, Chinese, other Asian and the Black Caribbean populations are moving out of the cities to the suburbs and more distant small towns. People of Pakistani and Bangladeshi origin remain very concentrated, but they too have become more dispersed.[33]

---

[30] David Coleman, *op. cit.,* pp. 22-7

[31] *Talk Money,* Barclay's Bank, May 2005, p. 20.

[32] See for example Harriet Bradley, Geraldine Healy & Nupur Mukherjee, 'Inclusion, Exclusion and Separate Organisation – Black Women Activists in Trade Unions', *Future of Work Series – Working Paper 25,* Leeds: ESRC Future of Work Programme, 2002, pp. 13-5.

[33] Daniel Dorling & Bethan Thomas, *People and Places: A 2001 Census atlas of the UK,* Bristol: Policy Press, 2004, p. 36.

However, other research shows that between 1993 and 2002 there was a net outflow of 606,000 people from London to other parts of the UK. Most of them were white. At the same time a net 726,000 immigrants arrived in London, many black. Often they settled in boroughs like Brent and Newham, where concentrations of Asian and African populations were already high.

If these trends persist, the concentration of ethnic groups could increase and Britain's white and ethnic minority populations would grow further apart.[34] With economic migration set to continue at historically high levels, how well will British people live together?

Migration is likely to strengthen the informal economy. For many people, 'informal is normal' has been true for a long time. The informal economy, defined as taxable activities that lie outside the tax regime, officially comprises 6.8% of the UK economy (though a number of estimates put the figure much higher).[35] It is dominated by tiny enterprises, family employment, small workshops and casual labour.

High levels of immigration will tend to bolster this sector. Migrant workers will continue to use informal channels to send some of their earnings back home. Low-paid casual workers will develop activities 'on the side' to tide them over between jobs and supplement their earnings in the formal economy.

Host communities will still have informal arrangements to help compatriots with transport to Britain, basic survival when they arrive and job searching. Migrants will commit a sizeable portion of their earnings to these activities. As now, some of these arrangements will border on the criminal, tying migrants into long periods of payment in a form of indentured labour.

Political pressure to limit migration may run up against the economy's need for more skills. If conditions for entry or permanent residency are tightened to meet public concerns, immigration could go 'under-ground'. More firms would turn to illegal sources of migrant labour, while the number of workers staying on illegally would increase. The criminal economy would grow.

Migration will bring mixed benefits to the countries of origin. On the upside, migration from the developing world will sometimes act as a safety valve. People with skills will find a job rather than be frustrated by the lack of local opportunities.

Remittances from migrants to families back home will be another plus. Current estimates suggest that, globally, remittances could be as high as £70 billion, more

---

[34] 'The Effect of Immigration on the Regions', http://www.migrationwatchuk.org/frameset. asp?menu=publications&page=publications.asp (accessed 1/3/05).
[35] Small Business Council, 'The Informal Economy', 2004, p. 8, http://www.sbs.gov.uk/content/sbc/informaleconomy.pdf.

than official aid.[36] The money can enable a family to build a better home, send a child to school or start a small business.

But the downsides will be considerable, too. The cost of transferring remittances can be as much as 20%, bring great benefits to middlemen but not to families receiving them.[37] The social costs of leaving home can be high. Children may not see their father or mother for several years, for example.

The migration of a country's brightest and best-educated young people may damage economic development. Health services in South Africa, especially in remote rural areas, are seriously at risk partly due to the 'brain drain' of health professionals. A shortage of professionals is the main constraint on improving health in sub-Saharan Africa.

What contribution will the UK make to managing the strains produced by global migration?

Points to take away

- Britain will rely more heavily on migrant workers, though they will be no labour market panacea.

- The number of Britons retiring abroad could prove a surprise, and create more space for immigrants to settle in the UK.

---

[36] 'Making the best of migration', *The Edge*, 18, March 2005, p. 13.
[37] Ibid, p. 13.

7. More workers from the edge of the labour market?

• Unemployment has fallen, but more men are inactive. Incapacity benefits claimants have tripled since 1979, but have declined since the mid '90s.

• Levels of inactivity should fall because older inactive people will retire in the next few years, the prevention and treatment of mental ill-health among workers will be a higher priority, and tools will exist to help disadvantaged people into jobs. But sufficient high-quality support is unlikely to be available.

• A sizeable core of adults will remain on the edge of the labour market. A long-term preventive approach, based on improving parenting skills, may be seen as one way forward.

More workers in their mid 60s and bullish levels of migration (at least for a while) will help to meet the continuing high demand for labour. In addition, government hopes that many on the edge of the labour market can be drawn into work, helping to lift the employment rate to about 80% of the working age population from almost 75% now.

Given the fall in registered unemployment, most of these extra workers will need to be people not actively seeking jobs at the moment. In particular, government aspires to shrink the total claiming incapacity benefits by as many as a million[1] - a large portion of the estimated 2.5 million additional workers needed to hit its 80% target.

In this chapter we concentrate on people with low educational attainment, and with a variety of physical and mental impairments. How many of them will be encouraged into jobs?

The story so far

Unemployment has fallen, but more men are inactive. The proportion of registered unemployed is now almost back to rates in the mid 1970s, but the proportion of inactive men – those who are not working and not officially unemployed – has remained stubbornly high.

---

[1] *Department for Work and Pensions Five Year Strategy. Opportunity and security throughout life,* cm 6447, London: the Stationery Office, 2005, pp. 25-7.

As Chart 7.1 shows, inactivity increased from 6.1% of working age men in 1973-76 to 16.1% in 2001-04. The figure for women dropped from 37.8% to 27.0%. More women are at work, but a growing number of men are not. (The employment of women is discussed in the next chapter.)

Chart 7.1 Unemployment has fallen, but more men are inactive, %

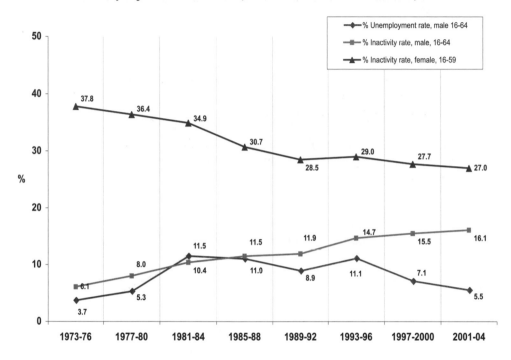

Source: ONS Labour Market Statistics – Integrated FR LFS TIME PERIODS, Tables YBTJ, YBTM, YBTN.

Notes:
(1) The inactive are those who are not working and not unemployed.
(2) The unemployed are those without a job who are looking for work in the reference week, or prevented from seeking work by temporary sickness or holiday, or waiting to start a job, or waiting for the results of a job application.
(3) All figures are UK, seasonally adjusted, four year averages.

In the late '90s and early 2000s, the employment rates of ethnic minorities born in Britain generally improved in relation to British-born whites. But Afro-Caribbean and Bangladeshi men were notable exceptions: their relative rates actually fell.[2]

---

[2] In the case of British-born Bengladeshi men, for example, from just under 65% in 1997 to 58% in 2002. Jonathan Wadsworth, 'The Labour Market Performance of Ethnic Minorities in the Recovery' in Richard Dickens, Paul Gregg & Jonathan Wadsworth (eds), *The Labour Market Under New Labour,* Basingstoke: Palgrave, 2003, pp. 119-25.

Although the Indian community contains almost as high a proportion of people in work as British-born whites, employment rates among other groups are lower, especially Bangladeshi and Pakistani women.

Inactivity rates of men are highest for 55 to 64 year olds, but have risen most sharply among lower-skilled men in the prime of life. The inactivity rate of men aged 55 to 64 had increased four fold by 2002, from 9.1% in 1972-6 to 34.5%, whereas the rate among men aged 25 to 54 had risen by almost seven times – from 1.1% to 7.5%.[3]

Between 50% and 60% of inactive prime-age men are in the bottom skill quartile, reflecting the deterioration of the low-skilled labour market in all industries. The Employment Service and medical gate-keepers have pushed unemployed men with chronic or long-term illness into a life on incapacity benefits, while more generous incapacity benefits than Jobseeker's Allowance has been a pull in the same direction. Around 70% of inactive men aged 25 to 54 report having a limiting health problem.[4]

The number claiming incapacity-related benefits has tripled since 1979, though figures have been falling since 1994-95. In 2004 the total was 2.7 million, most of them men. More adults report mental illness and behavioural disorders, while fewer are reporting physical impairments.[5]

'There are now more mentally ill people drawing incapacity benefits than there are unemployed people on Jobseeker's Allowance.'[6] At around 50%, the employment rate of disabled people is lower than for any other disadvantaged group, such as lone parents or black minority ethnic groups.[7]

Government policy has evolved in a 'social market' direction. Along with the US, New Zealand and Australia, in 1997 Britain's welfare system was based on free markets, with a social security 'floor' to protect individuals most in need. Since then, the government has injected a stronger social dimension into this market-based approach.

---

[3] Giulia Faggio & Stephen Nickell, 'The Rise in Inactivity Among Adult Men' in Richard Dickens, Paul Gregg & Jonathan Wadsworth (eds), *The Labour Market Under New Labour,* Basingstoke: Palgrave, 2003, pp. 42-3. The figures are based on the Labour Force Survey measurement of inactivity.

[4] Ibid, pp. 42-50.

[5] *Improving the Life Chances of Disabled People,* London: The Prime Minister's Strategy Unit, 2005, p. 33ff.

[6] Richard Layard, 'Mental Health: Britain's Biggest Social Problem?', paper presented to seminar hosted by the Prime Minister's Strategy Unit, 2004, http://www.strategy.gov.uk/downloads/files/mh_layard.pdf, p. 2.

[7] *Improving the Life Chances of Disabled People,* op. cit., pp. 32-3.

The cornerstone has been a greater emphasis on work as a route out of poverty. This has included tax credits and the National Minimum Wage to make work more rewarding, much heavier investment in education and training to equip individuals for employment, initiatives on child care to make it easier for mothers to work and a stronger insistence that, where appropriate, the right to welfare be matched by the responsibility to seek employment.

The New Deal for younger unemployed people, enshrining this approach, has been extended to lone parents and to older people. Personalised advice, job-related training and work experience, and the obligation to show commitment to the New Deal in return for benefits are important features of the programme. These same principles undergird the government's recently announced plans to help people on incapacity benefits into jobs where possible – plans that are likely to set the direction for policy over the next few years.

The next 20 years

Levels of inactivity should fall even without further government intervention. With inactivity highest among the older age group, the number of inactive people will decline as this age group retires. This will be a major driver behind reductions in the number claiming incapacity benefits over the next decade.

But partly offsetting this good news for inactivity will be significant levels of inactivity among younger adults. School-leavers with few qualifications will be the main reason. One in 20 school-leavers have no GCSE pass, and one in four 16 to 18 year olds had dropped out of education and training by the end of 2000.[8] Unless they augment their skills, they will find it difficult to get sustained employment as they grow older. As now, many will 'churn' through temporary jobs on the edge of the labour market. Some may drop out of the labour force completely.

In 2004, an estimated 7.7% of all England's 16 to 18 year olds were not in employment, education or training: they had no form of gainful activity.[9] Some have health problems and others live chaotic lives. Many lack the discipline and aptitude for work, damaging their employment prospects.

The number of children with mental and physical disabilities is on an upward trend. For children under 16, the total increased from 476,000 in 1975 to 772,000 in 2002, due probably to the greater prevalence of impairment among children, increased diagnosis, increased reporting and medical advances that enable children with complex conditions to live longer.[10] With most becoming adults, these children will swell the working-age population with impairments. Many will struggle to get jobs.

---

[8] *14-19 Opportuntiy and excellence,* London: DfES, 2003, pp. 4, 9.
[9] http://www.connexions.gov.uk/partnerships/documents/16-18%20NEET.xls (accessed 29/3/05).
[10] *Improving the Life Chances of Disabled People,* op.cit, p 26.

All in all, young adults with mental and physical disabilities will swell the ranks of inactive people. But the retirement of today's inactive older people will work in the opposite direction. Overall levels of inactivity should drop somewhat, even without further initiatives. Inactivity will shift from older adults to younger adults.

Workers' mental health will become a high priority. A 1998-99 study of 17,000 workers in Bristol found that a fifth of the sample reported occupational stress at 'very' or 'extremely' high levels. Follow-up interviews confirmed that high levels of work-related stress were significantly associated with ill-health, GP visits and accidents.[11] Acute stress forces some people out of work altogether.

In 2004, 38% of incapacity benefits recipients had mental health problems as their main disability, and mental problems were a secondary factor for 10% or more.[12] Workers with mental health problems cost the Exchequer an estimated £21 billion a year in lost taxes, support through public services and benefit payments.[13]

As cost pressures on government mount, cutting these costs will become urgent and spur further research into the nature of stress, its definition and measurement, and treatment. More support for people with depression and other mental illnesses will be available on the NHS, and employers will almost certainly be increasingly liable for work-induced stress. To avoid litigation and control absenteeism, organisations will develop new techniques to address the problem.

Have we already begun to turn the corner? The Health and Safety Executive's occupational health surveillance data suggests that work-related stress increased between 1995 and 2001/02, but has levelled off since (and may even have declined).[14] Nearly two-fifths of managers surveyed in 2002 reported that they had reviewed working practices to avoid occupational stress or were doing so.[15] Workplace injuries have fallen by over 10% since 1997.[16]

---

[11] Andrew Smith, Sarbjit Johal, Emma Wadsworth, George Davey Smith & Tim Peters, *The Scale of Occupational Stress. The Bristol Stress and Health at Work Study,* London: HMSO, 2000, pp. 21-8, 135-49.

[12] Richard Layard, *op. cit.,* p. 6.

[13] Ibid, p. 8.

[14] http:/www.hse.gov.uk/statistics/causdis/stress.htm (accessed 29/3/05).

[15] Robert Taylor, *Managing Workplace Change,* ESRC Future of Work Programme Seminar Series, n.d., p. 15.

[16] *Department for Work and Pensions Five Year Strategy.* op. cit., p. 43.

Global competition and continuous innovation will increase demands on workers and create conditions in which they feel stressed.[17] But at the same time, controlling stress will move further up the health and safety agenda.

Tools will exist to support disadvantaged people into work. Job coaching under the New Deal, for example, can involve mentors working with disabled people to discover their capabilities. The mentor may work in an available job, learn the required skills, sit alongside the disabled person to pass on those skills and then gradually withdraw as the disabled person gains confidence.

Government has been trialling other personalised approaches in its 'Pathways to Work' pilots. At the heart of these pilots is a personal adviser who provides monthly contact in the early stages of a claim for incapacity benefit. The adviser puts the individual in touch with NHS support, which includes 'condition management' to help the person return to work. A £40 a week back-to-work credit is paid to people who get a job. The number of incapacity benefit claimants returning to work in the pilot districts has doubled.[18]

Government intends gradually to extend Pathways across the country, as part of a package to encourage people with mental and physical impairments into employment. It expects to pilot the placement of employment advisers in GPs' surgeries, so that advice on managing health and managing steps back to employment can be more closely integrated. It plans to reform incapacity benefits. Claimants will receive benefit at a higher level than the Jobseeker's Allowance only if they engage in work-focused interviews and activities that prepare them for employment. All the evidence shows that the longer people are off work, the less likely they are to return to work.

Disadvantaged younger people will be encouraged into work through initiatives such as the proposed pilot for 14 to 16 year olds involving a tailored programme for each young person, intensive personal guidance and support, and work-based learning, probably amounting to two days a week.[19] Time will tell whether the government's intended rationalisation of vocational training within a new Diploma framework will prove effective in raising the skills of less academic young people.

---

[17] For links between competition, innovation and work effort see Francis Green & Steven McIntosh, *Working on the Chain Gang? An Examination of Rising Effort Levels in Europe in the 1990s,* London: LSE Centre for Economic Performance, Discussion Paper 465, 2000.

[18] *Department for Work and Pensions Five Year Strategy.* op. cit., p. 45.

[19] *14-19 Education and Skills,* cm 6476, London: The Stationery Office, 2005, pp. 50-59, 70-1.

Education Maintenance Allowances, paid to 16 to 19 year olds from poor backgrounds who continue with academic or vocational learning, are thought to have increased participation in pilot areas by 5.9%. Now available across the country, from April 2006 they will be supplemented by 'activity allowances' for 16 and 17 year olds not in employment or learning.[20] Both could prove significant policy levers. Raising the allowances and increasing the bonus for those who stay on their course could strengthen the incentive to keep learning.

A new policy framework is emerging, based on personalised support and financial incentives. Elements within this framework will be developed in the light of experience and new ones added, with greater attention being paid to the prevention and treatment of mental ill-health.

A range of technologies will support this approach. Large screen monitors, voice recognition software, alternative keyboards and other supportive technologies will make many jobs more friendly to people with physical impairments. For example, a computer controlled by brainpower alone has allowed a severely disabled British man to type out a message just by thinking.[21]

Learning wrapped up in computer games may prove effective in helping disaffected young people acquire life skills and essential qualifications, especially as more sophisticated software is developed. Already LearnDirect provides computer-based numeracy courses in bite-sized chunks. In time such courses will have a stronger 'games' element, so that the distinction between fun and learning is blurred.

One model used in the voluntary sector is to allow truants to play computer games for as long as they like. Youth workers gradually build relationships with the young people, encouraging them to supplement computer games with computer-based learning and teaching them life skills informally. Eventually some of the young people are 'mentored' back to school or college, or into employment.

'Soft' technologies to treat anxiety and other common forms of mental disorder will continue to be developed. Cognitive behavioural therapy – sometimes in conjunction with drugs – has been shown to be highly effective among the majority of clients, and has even doubled the rate at which unemployed people find work.[22]

---

[20] *14-19 Education and Skills,* op. cit., p 69.
[21] *The Sunday Times,* 29 April 2001.
[22] Richard Layard, *op. cit.,* pp. 8-9.

Sufficient high-quality support is unlikely to be available, however. An estimated 10,000 extra psychological therapists would be required to make a large dent on mental illness in the workforce. This would include a doubling of the number of clinical psychologists in training, which would take time to achieve.[23]

Personalised support for people with mental and physical illness is labour-intensive. It requires advisers with high-order interpersonal skills. The nuances can be quite subtle, such as distinguishing quickly between individuals who want to be told what to do ('it's all so complicated, you tell me what to do') and those who prefer support in developing their own return-to-work strategies.

The Department of Work and Pensions has acknowledged the challenge of improving the quality of its personalised advice while cutting 30,000 equivalent full-time posts by 2008, as part of the Gershon efficiency drive across Whitehall.[24]

Yet perhaps more problematic for government and its voluntary and private sector partners will be finding staff with sufficient skills. One report noted that the multiplication of initiatives for underachieving boys and young men was hitting a shortage of people willing and able to work with them.[25]

The shortage could worsen because individuals with skills to be effective personal advisers will be in great demand, not least to fill the burgeoning number of customer-facing jobs in the expanding service sector. Many of these service jobs will become more skilled to meet rising consumer expectations. Will government and other agencies be able to afford well-qualified advisers? And if not, will poor practice bring new personalised approaches into disrepute?

Many programmes, like those which encourage disaffected young people into work, require employer support. Some employers will co-operate out of commitment to social responsibility, and increasingly perhaps to secure much-needed labour. But others will be reluctant to devote management time to individuals with behavioural or physical needs. Will they prefer the alternative of moving abroad, turning to illegal migrants or investing in labour saving equipment?

Financial incentives such as the Education Maintenance Allowance may have limited impact at current levels, especially for the most disaffected people. Will resources be available to make these financial carrots more tasty? Or will the public be indifferent to marginal groups, preventing higher levels of spending, or grow resentful even and demand that spending be cut?

---

[23] Richard Layard, *op. cit.,* p.17, 21-2.

[24] *Department for Work and Pensions Five Year Strategy.* op. cit., p. 68.

[25] 'A school-based programme to prepare underachieving young men for work', *Findings,* York: JRF, September 2002.

Suitable jobs for those on the edge of the labour market may be hard to find. Many of the long-term sick live in areas, often Northern cities, with relatively few job opportunities. 'The geography of permanent sickness' became more entrenched in the 1990s, with rates rising most where they were highest to begin with.[26] Encouraging individuals to travel a long distance to available jobs, let alone move home, is fraught with difficulty.

The long-term sick and out-of-work tend to have few skills, and have often lost – or never had – the disciplines necessary for work. Yet as the UK moves up the value chain, even relatively unskilled jobs will become more demanding. Shoppers will check out their own purchases, for example, perhaps permitting check-out staff to become shopping advisers.

As more skills are expected of those in employment, work risks pulling further away from low-skilled people without jobs. Will individuals on the fringe of the labour market be able to run faster to catch up?

What might be the implications?

Measures to increase participation in work will have mixed results. The total receiving incapacity benefits will fall in the next few years because many will retire. Better prevention and more treatment, mostly in the next decade, will cut the number of workers leaving employment through work-related stress.

But there will continue to be many young people who are ill-equipped for work. The tools for helping them into employment are being developed, but will there be enough resources? A sizeable core of adults with multiple disadvantages will probably remain on the edge of the labour market.

Policy objectives are likely to clash. On the one hand, tight labour markets and the desire to reduce low pay could maintain pressure to lift the National Minimum Wage at a faster rate than pay generally. As we have seen, this could force employers at the bottom end gradually to shift into higher-skilled methods of production, requiring fewer workers.[27]

---

[26] Daniel Dorling & Bethan Thomas, *People and places. A 2001 Census atlas of the UK,* Bristol: Policy Press, 2004, p. 93.

[27] In hairdressing, for example, though salon-owners tended either to absorb the additional costs of the NMW or pass it on in higher prices, research found evidence of some innovation in management practice in response to the NMW, such as greater cost control, use of appraisals, fast-tracking for trainees and monitoring attendance. Janet Druker, Celia Stanworth & Geoffrey White, *Report to the Low Pay Commission on the Impact of the National Minimum Wage on the Hairdressing Sector,* London: Work & Research Unit University of Greenwich Business School, 2003, pp. 41-53.

On the other hand, this would lengthen ladders into work for those on the edge of the labour market. Fewer jobs would exist for people with very low skills. Achieving the government's aspiration of an 80% employment rate would become more difficult.

Adding to the tension could be the interests of an overheating London economy, which might force the minimum wage to levels increasingly out of line with labour market conditions in slower growing parts of Britain. Job prospects would suffer for inactive people who are more likely to live in these slow growth regions and are least likely to move to more dynamic areas. Might regional or local variations in the minimum wage eventually come on to the agenda, despite their practical difficulties?

Action to prevent people sliding to the labour market fringe is widely seen as vital. Preventive measures at any stage are helpful, but ideally they should start at the beginning of life. Writing about children with mental and physical impairments, the Prime Minister's Strategy Unit noted,

> 'The early years are a critical period for disabled children. Child development and future life chances – as well as those of siblings – are critically affected by the support and services received by young disabled children and their families. Targeting support at these families will also play a major role in helping to eradicate child poverty.'[28]

Children from low income households are more prone to report long standing illness, disability or mental health problems. They are more likely to be low birth weight, for example, with the associated risk of delayed motor and social development, and other health problems.[29] Childhood poverty (including being brought up in care) increases the risk of poor educational attainment and poor employment in later life.

Effective support in the early years could bring large savings in public spending. One study found that by age 28, on average each 10 year old with severe behaviour problems (2.8% of the age group) cost the state an extra £70,019 above the basic universal provision. Those with less severe conduct problems (9.2% of the age group) cost an additional £24,324.[30]

---

[28] *Improving the Life Chances of Disabled People,* op. cit., p. 85.

[29] Ibid, p. 86.

[30] These costs (in 1998 prices) exclude private, voluntary agency, indirect and personal costs. Stephen Scott, Martin Knapp, Juliet Henderson, Barbara Maughan, 'Financial cost of social exclusion: follow up study of antisocial children into childhood', *British Medical Journal,* 323, 2001, pp. 1-5.

Government attaches a high priority in its health, education and inclusion strategies to early intervention, such as the Sure Start programme. It is beginning to provide support for parents, such as videos and guides on how to help their children with reading or maths. Some primary schools are going further, exploring how they can provide parenting classes (not under that name) to improve the quality of parental support for children.

Other schools are developing innovative ways of helping children with emotional and behavioural difficulties. One approach is to create a special, attractive room for young children who disrupt their class. Small groups have family-like meals together and receive special attention. The aim is to create a family environment in which children can receive the love they missed at home. After a few weeks, the children are encouraged back to their classrooms, often in a calmer state. These kinds of approach will continue to spread.

As they do, the perception may strengthen that improving the quality of parenting can shield children from the worst effects of social and economic disadvantage. Poverty and other disadvantages are largely mediated through parents. Research shows that it is fairly simple and inexpensive to train parents in child management skills, and that many children with behaviour disorders respond well.[31]

Might a consensus emerge that early action to train parents – and compensate for poor parenting – could prove one of the most effective ways of improving the life chances and employability of disadvantaged young people?

Points to take away

• Drawing people on the edge of the labour market into employment will have some success, but not enough skilled support may be available.

• Might attention focus more strongly on prevention, including measures to combat work-related stress, with even more emphasis on the early years and improving the quality of parenting?

---

[31] For example, Carole Sutton, 'Training Parents to Manage Difficult Children: A Comparison of Methods', *Behavioural Psychotherapy,* 1992, 20, pp. 115-39; Stephen Scott, Quentin Spender, Moira Doolan, Brian Jacobs, Helen Aspland, 'Multicentre controlled trial of parenting groups for childhood antisocial behaviour in clinical practice', *British Medical Journal,* 323, 2001, pp. 11-17.

8. Better opportunities for women?

> • Job segregation, the effects of having children and women's preferences continue to leave women at a disadvantage in the labour market.
>
> • Better-educated women, a stronger desire among mothers to combine work with young children, tight labour markets and a greater commitment by employers to diversity will increase gender equality at work.
>
> • More women could be in full-time employment, the earnings gap between men and women will narrow further and the woman will earn more than the man in a larger number of couples, with implications for the wider society.

Possibly the most significant social development since World War II has been the growing number of women at work. Women now comprise almost half the UK workforce. The employment rate for women (69% in 2004 against 79% for men) is the highest recorded in modern times.[1]

Single-earner households, with men as the breadwinners, have evolved into dual earner households, in which the man is generally the main earner and the woman has the secondary income. But women are now breaking through into more senior management positions, and earning more than their partners in 11% of couples.[2]

Might greater equality be on the way, with perhaps even a reversal of gender inequalities on the horizon as more women reach the top of organisations and have larger pay packets than their partners?

The story so far

Britain's workplaces are clearly very different to those of the early 1970s. The Equal Pay Act came into force in 1975 and provided for equal pay for men and women doing 'like work' for the same employer. The Sex Discrimination Act in 1975 provided for the equal treatment of men and women in most spheres. The Equal Opportunities Commission, established under the Act, has established codes of practice that have shaped most organisations' equal opportunity policies.

Both these Acts have been strengthened over the years, not least as a result of initiatives from the EU. Yet despite this legislative framework, three barriers to gender equality at work have persisted.

---

[1] ONS LFS Time Series Tables FR9, Table YBTJ. Updated 03/05.

[2] Michael Willmott & William Nelson, *Complicated Lives,* London: Wiley, 2003, p. 133. Some of these 11% will be partnerships in which the man has lost his job or been forced on to Incapacity Benefit.

Job segregation

The first is the segregation of jobs by sex. When certain categories of job are filled mainly by men or women, women's ability to take advantage of anti-discrimination legislation is weakened: if fewer women are working alongside men in the same kinds of employment, it is harder to prove that jobs are of a comparable nature and deserve equal pay.

The gender segregation of jobs still exists. Care assistants, sales checkout staff and 'dinner ladies' in schools are examples of occupations that are held mainly by women, are low-paid and have few prospects. Women have traditionally dominated nursing and primary school teaching, which pay modest salaries compared to other professions. In parts of manufacturing, an assembly department may be all female, while the next-door machining department is entirely male. Public services employ women in nearly three jobs out of every four, while engineering and construction employ one in five.[3]

Women are still concentrated in part-time jobs. In 2004, 44.1% of the 13 million women over 16 in employment worked part-time against only 10.6% of men.[4] Part-time employment in turn is concentrated in specific workplaces and industries, such as hotels, catering and retailing, and often in occupations utilising low-skilled methods of production.[5] This occupational concentration accounts for the low pay and poor conditions of many part-time jobs rather than the part-time status itself.

But the situation today is much better than it was, despite the persistence of job segregation. Three decades ago most jobs were segregated. Now, women have prised open many occupations that had been closed to them. For example:

- In 1964 one in five qualified practising pharmacists was a woman: by 2001 this had risen to a half.[6] The pattern is similar in other professions, such medicine and law.

- Women in business services, a powerhouse of the British economy, increased from 42% of jobs in 1971 to 48% in 1999, at a time when the sector grew from 12% of all employment to 24%.[7]

---

[3] Michael White, Stephen Hill, Colin Mills & Deborah Smeaton, *Managing to Change?*, Basingstoke: Palgrave, 2004, p. 104.

[4] ONS Labour Market Statistics – Integrated FR LFS TIME PERIODS, Tables YCBI, YCBJ, MGSA, MGSB.

[5] Sonia Liff, 'The Industrial Relations of a Diverse Workforce' in Paul Edwards (ed), *Industrial Relations: Theory and Practice,* Oxford: Blackwell, 2003, p. 431.

[6] Michael White, Stephen Hill, Colin Mills and Deborah Smeaton, *op. cit.,* p. 103.

[7] Ibid, p. 196.

• The proportion of managers who are women leapt from a mere eight per cent in 1990 to a quarter in the early 2000s.[8]

A 2002 survey of managers at 2000 workplaces found that job segregation continued to be eroded.

• In the previous 12 months 15% of workplaces had recruited men into hitherto all-female jobs, and 18% had recruited women into all-male jobs.

• One in four workplaces had made a change in one or both directions, while one in four said that the questions did not apply to them because they already had no jobs that were all-male or all-female.

• About a half of the workplaces had recently done, or were doing something toward desegregating employment between men and women.[9]

Mothers get left behind

The second barrier to gender equality at work is the interaction between employment and family life. Mothers who stop work to look after a child often miss out on promotion, and fail to accumulate skills and experience that would boost their earnings later on. Women who combine work and motherhood (especially when their children are very young) earn more than mothers who don't.[10]

Though female activity rates have risen, they have not yet caught up with men. The proportion of women in employment or looking for jobs rose from 62.2% in 1973-76 to 73.0% in 2001-4 (Chart 8.1). Despite this, at 83.9% in 2004 the activity rate for working-age men was more than ten per cent above the rate for women.[11]

---

[8] Michael Willmott & William Nelson, *op. cit.,* p. 131.

[9] Michael White, Stephen Hill, Colin Mills and Deborah Smeaton, *op. cit.,* pp. 106-7.

[10] Helen Robinson, 'Gender and Labour Market Performance in the Recovery' in Richard Dickens, Paul Gregg & Jonathan Wadsworth (eds), *The Labour Market Under New Labour,* Biasingstoke: Palgrave, *2003,* p. 243.

[11] Michael White, Stephen Hill, Colin Mills and Deborah Smeaton, *op. cit.,* p. 103.

Chart 8.1 Female activity rates have risen (women aged 16-59, UK seasonally adjusted, four year averages; %)

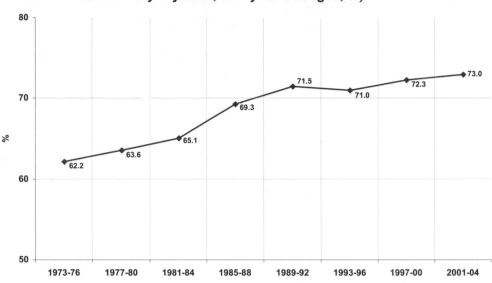

Source: ONS LFS Time Series Tables FR9, Tables YBTM, YBTN. Updated 03/05.

The main reason why fewer women are employed is the effect of having children, illustrated in Table 8A. This is especially true of single mothers. In 2002 only 51% of single parents (usually mothers) with children aged 16 and under were at work, significantly less than for all women with children that age. The proportion was substantially higher, however, than the 39% figure in 1993.[12]

Table8A. Fewer women work when their children are young. (% of women at work by age of child in 2002)

0-1	2-3	4-5	6-7	8-16	16+	No children
50	54	63	70	74	77	77

Source: Helen Robinson, 'Gender and Labour Market Performance in the Recovery' op. cit., p 236.

Note: Figures, based on Labour Force Survey, include women on unemployment schemes and exclude students.

---

[12] Helen Robinson, *op.cit,* p. 237.

Mothers wanting to work are at a smaller disadvantage than they used to be, despite the effects of having children.

> • Changing attitudes, coupled with legislation to extend maternity and more recently paternity rights, have made it easier for women to combine motherhood with employment. In 1979 one in four women employees resumed paid work roughly within a year of having a baby. By the mid 1990s, the proportion had jumped to two thirds.[13]

> • Employers have continued to extend family-friendly policies (though with a narrow range of options). The 2002 survey found that many employers (especially in retailing) had made it easier for women to switch from full to part-time work and back again, and that a significant number had introduced bundles of family-friendly measures.[14]

> • Flexible working has extended further since April 2003, when parents with children under age six, or with disabled children under 18, were given the statutory right to request flexible work. The organisation, Working Families, found that by March 2004 two-fifths of its members and parents seeking advice (admittedly a slanted sample) had made a request. Sixty per cent of these requests had been granted.[15] Most requests were for part-time work, or to start late and/or leave early.[16]

> • Thanks largely to women finding it easier to combine children with employment, the average (mean) gender pay gap has continued to narrow gradually, from 26% in 1997 to 23% in 2002.[17]

Women's preferences

The preferences of women themselves are a third influence on gender equality at work. In a representative sample of over three and a half thousand persons aged 16 and over, just 17% of women would prefer to focus their time and energy on home

---

[13] Michael White, Stephen Hill, Colin Mills and Deborah Smeaton, *op. cit.,* p. 4.

[14] Ibid, pp 110-114.

[15] Working Families, *Right to Request Flexible Working: Review of impact in first year of legislation,* 2004, http://www.workingfamilies.org.uk/asp/employer_zone/reports/R2R_Report_March2004.doc.

[16] *A parent's right to ask: A review of flexible working arrangements,* 2003, http://www.cipd.co.uk/subjects/wrkgtime/flexwking/prntrighttoask.htm?IsSrchRes=1.

[17] Helen Robinson, *op.cit,* pp. 239-42.

and family work. Just 14% were 'work-centred' – having a strong commitment to paid employment and regarding themselves as the joint main earner with their partner. The great majority, 69%, fell into a compromise model in which women were either the secondary earner or did not view employment as central to their lives.

Different lifestyle preferences had a substantial impact on the actual employment choices of women. Preferences predicted participation rates, but the latter did not predict preferences. Causation was one-way: from women's core values to their employment choices, not the other way round. The impact of lifestyle preferences was stronger than the impact of education.

Women are to be found in part-time and lower-paid jobs not just because of institutional barriers to equality, but also because many women are content to take this form of work. These jobs match their willingness to be the secondary earner and to avoid making work central to their lives.[18]

A long way to go

Job segregation, the employment effects of motherhood and women's preferences mean that a long journey remains to full equal opportunities at work.

> • A half of all workplaces in the 2002 survey still had jobs that were exclusively for men or women, yet had taken no recent steps to recruit the opposite sex into them.[19]

> • The gender pay gap is narrowing only slowly. It has narrowed modestly for women in full-time work (women earned 18% less than men in 1994 and 15% less in 2002), but not for part timers, for whom the gap has remained at 36%.[20] According to one study, a typical woman with GCSE qualifications in the UK earns £241,000 less than her male counterpart over a lifetime simply on the basis of gender. Having children adds another £140,000 to the loss.[21]

> • Two-fifths (44%) of employed women in Great Britain worked part-time in Spring 2004, largely because of family responsibilities, against 11% of men. According to the Equal Opportunities Commission, hourly wages increase by 3% for each year of full-time employment, but they decrease by 1% for each year of part-time work.[22]

---

[18] Catherine Hakim, 'Sex Differences in Work-Life Balance Goals' in Diane M Houston (ed.), *Work-Life Balance in the 21st Century,* Basingstoke: Palgrave, 2005, pp. 59-71.
[19] Michael White, Stephen Hill, Colin Mills and Deborah Smeaton, *op. cit.,* p. 107.
[20] Helen Robinson, *op. cit.,* p. 241.
[21] Cited by Sonia Liff, *op. cit.,* p.436.
[22] *Part-time is no crime – so why the penalty?*, London: Equal Opportunities Commission, 2005, pp. 21, 24.

• More women are managers than in the past, but this has been largely due to the widespread re-designation of lower level jobs as managerial.[23] Men still dominate the most senior positions. In 2002, 81% of corporate managers were male.[24] The following year, almost 92% of the FTSE 100 companies' board members were also male.[25]

• Although mothers are returning to work more quickly after child-birth, for many juggling home and a career feels like an impossible task. Many are strongly dissatisfied with their work-life balance. Chart 8.2 shows that women's satisfaction with their hours of work fell sharply between 1992 and 2000.

Chart 8.2 Working women are more dissatisfied with their hours (% completely or very satisfied with hours worked)

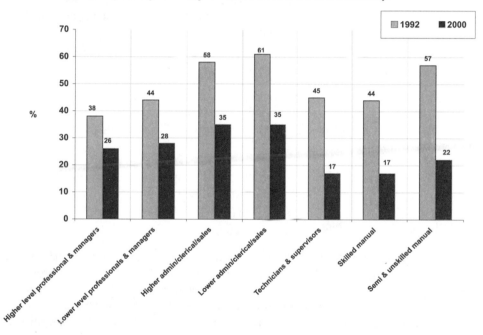

Source: Robert Taylor, *Diversity in Britain's Labour Market,* ESRC Future of Work Seminar Series, Swindon: ESRC, 2003, p. 16.

---

[23] Data from the Workplace Employment Relations Survey suggests that between 1990 and 1999, two-fifths of establishments increased their management posts by over 50%. A quarter of women managers described their daily tasks as involving non-managerial work in routine administration and sales. Irene Bruegel, 'Seeking the Critical Mass: Quantitative and Qualitative Aspects of the Feminisation of Management in Britain in the 1990s' in Paul Stewart (ed.), *Employment, Trade Union Renewal and the Future of Work,* Basingstoke: Palgrave, 2004, pp. 95-6, 112.

[24] Helen Robinson, *op. cit.,* p. 239.

[25] Cranfield University School of Management, *The 2003 Female FTSE Index,* http://www.som.cranfield.ac.uk/som/ccdwbl/downloads/FTSEIndex2003.apdf (accessed 10/11/04).

The next 20 years

Four factors will influence the amount of progress made toward gender equality at work over the coming two decades.

The first will be women's educational attainment. Women overtook men at every level of education in the 1990s. For example, in 1990 women accounted for 45% of undergraduates and 41% of postgraduates: in 2000 there were five women undergraduates for every four men, and more women than men at postgraduate level. In the EU as a whole, the predominance of women in higher education is equally pronounced.[26] Girls are also out-performing boys in GCSEs and A-levels.

This means that among young people entering the workforce, more women than men will be qualified for the best jobs. At present, women are disproportionately represented among the low-paid largely because older women have fewer qualifications. If women continue to outperform men at school and university, eventually more women will be competing for the better jobs.

As higher university fees kick in, women graduates may become more committed to employment to secure a return on their investment – 'why accumulate all this debt if I don't fly to the heights my degree allows?' They may delay having children, or return to work more quickly afterwards.

Will women's superior education force a growing number to have partners who are less educated than they are? At present, successful women seek to avoid marrying down, and look for partners who will not expect the woman to pick up all the bills.[27] But might this begin to change?

US research shows that highly-educated women are less likely than in the past to feel the need to marry men who are more successful than they are. Their preference to marry better-educated men had all but disappeared by 2000. Well-educated women had not flooded the market and reduced the number of marriages, as some commentators expected. Rather, the market adjusted to the increased supply of educated women.[28]

On this basis, if there are 20% more women undergraduates in Britain than men, for example, some of these women will 'couple up' with men who are not graduates. In time, they will earn more than their partners. US wives who are better-educated than their husbands are one and a half times as likely to earn more than their husbands as to earn the same.[29]

---

[26] Michael Willmott & William Nelson, *op. cit.*, p. 131.

[27] Catherine Hakim, 'Sex Differences in Work-Life Balance Goals' in Diane M Houston (ed.), *Work-Life Balance in the 21st Century,* Basingstoke: Palgrave, 2005, p. 66.

[28] *The Futurist,* July-August 2004, p. 20. The research reported was undertaken by economist Elaina Rose at the University of Washington.

[29] Sara B. Raley et al, 'How Dual are Dual-Income Couples? Documenting Change from 1970 to 2001', paper presented at 2003 American Sociological Association meeting, August 15-19, Atlanta, Georgia, p. 21.

Secondly, more mothers will probably combine work and children, continuing the current trend. Deciding whether and when to have children involves a complex trade-off. In particular, the desire to have a family has to be set against the economic costs – the loss of earnings if one partner spends some time out of the labour market, or the costs of childcare if the mother returns to work quickly, and of course the extra cost of children themselves (estimated in 1997 at about £50,000 per child till age 17 [30]).

Prospective parents also bring into the equation their notion of what good parenting involves. If they think that it is best for the mother to look after the child in the early years, quickly returning to work will be less of an option. The choice becomes more stark – parenting versus job.

At present women's views are still quite traditional, leaning towards 'motherhood means staying at home to begin with'. A slight majority of younger women still say they would be happy to stay at home if their partner earned more, and only one in four say they would prefer the role of breadwinner.

But at the same time, these younger women are significantly more likely to reject the role of housewife than those who are older. Remarkably, six out of ten men say they would be happy to accept the role of househusband if their partner was the chief income earner.[31] Traditional views are on the wane – slowly.

Women's preferences are likely to shift further toward work. Better-educated women, encouraged by skill shortages and employer commitment to diversity, will break into higher-paid and more responsible jobs. As discussed in chapter 15, state-supported childcare provision will improve, making it easier to combine employment and motherhood. Work will become more attractive compared to staying at home.

As this happens, assumptions about motherhood are likely to continue their slow evolution. Women often adjust their expectations in response to labour market opportunities. A study of 34 young mothers in Milton Keynes found that some women who thought that you could not be good mother and work full-time modified that view when they themselves got full-time jobs.[32]

For a growing number of young women in better-paid employment, being a 'good' mother will not mean staying at home while the children are young, but being 'savvy' in choosing the best childcare. Mothers will make work a more central feature of their lives and be less satisfied with second-rate employment.

---

[30] Sue Middleton, Karl Ashworth & Ian Braithwaite, 'Expenditure on children in Great Britain', *Findings*, York: Joseph Rowntree Foundation, 1997. A poll of 500 parents for the online bank, Egg, came to roughly the same figure in 2004. http://bbc.news.co.uk/1/hi/education/4003263.stm (accessed 14/12/04).
[31] Michael Willmott & William Nelson, *op. cit.*, p. 133.
[32] Susan Himmelweit & Maria Sigala, 'Choice and the Relationship between Identity and Behaviour for Mothers with Pre-School Children: Some implications for Policy from a UK Study', *Journal of Social Policy,* 33(3), 2004, pp. 455-78.

Thirdly, the persistence of tight labour markets will encourage employers to knock down barriers to the employment of women. Organisations that are desperate for labour will have little truck with segregation if it hinders recruitment. Presumably it is no coincidence that the quarter of workplaces recruiting the opposite sex into traditionally segregated jobs in the 2002 survey did so when skill shortages were becoming more acute.[33]

As we have seen, tight labour markets may also make it easier to haul up the National Minimum Wage faster than pay increases generally, benefiting the disproportionate number of women on low pay. Again, it may be no coincidence that the minimum wage has outpaced average pay increases since 1999, just when many labour markets were tightening.[34] This has helped to cut modestly the pay gap between men and women among low-paid workers.[35]

Finally, employers' commitment to diversity is likely to grow, and this will influence their treatment of women. The business case for diversity is gaining ground. A diverse workforce helps organisations relate to the variety of groups in society, aids innovation by extending the range of views among employees and can strengthen the organisation's reputation. This case will be reinforced by regulation, which is likely to become more stringent.

At the same time, human resource management (HRM) will become more sophisticated to avoid litigation in an increasingly litigious society, to manage repeated change as firms move into higher-skilled activities, to train employees for more skilled jobs and to retain workers in whom the organisation has invested. HRM specialists will play a more central role, and become more influential as a result.

Strong employer commitment to HRM is often associated with family-friendly initiatives. HR specialists tend to be sensitive to the issues involved and can resource the implementation of new policies. A generous approach to the work-life balance increasingly forms part of a broader strategy to make the organisation an employer of choice.[36] As HR managers' influence grows, more organisations will put equal opportunities for women at the heart of their employment practices.

---

[33] Michael White, Stephen Hill, Colin Mills and Deborah Smeaton, *op. cit.*, p. 106.

[34] The Minimum Wage increased by 35% in its first five years (1999-2004), whereas pay grew by 2.6% a year on average. Donald Hirsch, 'Trends in poverty and inequality', *Prospect*, May 2004, p. 48.

[35] Helen Robinson, *op. cit.*, pp. 245-6.

[36] Shirley Dex & Colin Smith, *The nature and pattern of family-friendly employment policies in Britain,* Bristol: Policy Press, 2002, p. 14.

What might be the implications?

Better employment opportunities for women could boost the labour supply. Better-educated women, a shifting assessment of the relative merits of work and full-time motherhood, tight labour markets and greater employer commitment to diversity could pull down the barriers to gender equality at work and gradually expand the career openings available to women.

As a result, a growing minority of women may find employment a more attractive alternative to motherhood (which would be bad news for Britain's low birth rate). Mothers may return to work more quickly. Might women become more reluctant to take part-time work? This could improve the labour supply significantly. Instead of the equivalent of one full-time job being done by two people, it would require only one.

The earnings gap between men and women will continue to narrow, if slowly. More couples will earn roughly the same. In the United States, the proportion of such couples nearly tripled from 9% in 1970 to 24% in 2001.[37] The minority of couples in which women earn more than men will also grow.

As more women earn much the same as (or more than) their partners, many couples will find themselves substantially well off. Among the many ramifications, they will find it easier to pay for childcare, cleaning and other domestic services that will help both partners to work full-time. Will fewer women (and men) want part-time jobs?

They will also be able to spend more on their homes. Given a tight housing supply, will this drive house prices even higher? Might couples with both partners working not feel as well off as their joint incomes warrant because they will be spending more on their mortgages?

Where both partners are earning much the same, couples will have an incentive to distribute the household chores more equally. If both are contributing equally to the household budget, it will seem natural that childcare and other domestic tasks should be shared evenly too. As has begun gradually to happen, greater equality at work will feed through – though slowly – to greater equality at home, and this will influence the expectations of the next generation.

Might we see more role reversals, encouraged by the increasing minority of couples in which the woman earns more than the man? If the couple cannot afford childcare or make arrangements with family or friends, it will make economic sense for the man to become a househusband or work part-time. As more couples choose these options, they will become possibilities for others and the trend will steadily accelerate. This will be a big change from today, where role reversals are

---

[37] Sara B. Raley et al, *op,cit*, p. 15.

often enforced by job insecurity, job loss or ill-health.[38]

As opportunities at work become more equal, a larger number of women could move into more senior positions. Today's slow trend in this direction may speed up. Many of these more senior women will be instinctively sympathetic to measures that will help women combine their caring responsibilities with employment. More women bosses will push forward equal opportunities.

This will be despite the discouraging evidence to date. Women in management 'appear neither to be in positions to "grow" more female managers to work alongside them, nor to influence decisively the opportunities open to other women…women managers continue to operate largely as individuals in a man's world.'[39] More women in positions of responsibility could well change this. A 'tipping point' may occur as a larger number of women reach senior positions, and champion family-friendly measures and other 'feminine' values.

Greater gender equality at work would help to create a more equal balance of power between the sexes generally. This will be because economic power lies behind many other forms of power. How might the rebalancing of gender power at work and then at home affect society more widely? Will the 'feminisation' of culture accelerate, for example, with traditional preoccupations of women (like emotions) continuing to be more valued? Or will men and women become more similar – the age of androgyny that some predict?

Finally, these trends will add to the complexity of life. As opportunities become more equal, the possibilities for mixing work and home will get more numerous. Will both partners work full-time, or will they both look for part-time jobs, or will the father work part-time and the mother full-time, and so on? More options will have to be negotiated. Yet couples will be less able to draw on traditional expectations to guide them. Relationships will become even more complicated.

Points to take away

• Opportunities at work will become more equal, not least because women will be better qualified and employers will be strapped for skills.

• The number of couples where both partners earn roughly the same will increase, and this will impact the balance of influence between the sexes.

---

[38] For example, see Nickie Charles, Emma James & Paul Ransome, 'Perceptions of Job Insecurity in a Retail Sector Organisation' in Paul Stewart (ed.), *Employment, Trade Union Renewal and the Future of Work,* Basingstoke: Palgrave, 2004, p. 182.

[39] Irene Bruegel, *op. cit.,* p. 113.

How will work be organised?

9. How far will individuals work for themselves?

- There has been no clear trend to self-employment since the mid 1990s, nor to employment in micro-companies (which can feel similar to self-employment).

- Future trends will be influenced by the value society attaches to the personal, the relative power of the corporate sector, the opportunities created by electronic networks and the search for stability, which may reduce individuals' willingness to take risks.

- Individualised work may not replace the corporate workplace as quickly as some have thought. This will have implications for policies to encourage enterprise and skills.

In the 1980s and '90s it was widely thought that the distinction between employment and self-employment would break down. More people would work for themselves rather than for someone else, in a variety of contractual relationships.[1] In 'the new world of work', self-employment would play a crucial role. Do recent trends bear this out?

The story so far

At one stage, a steady rise in self-employment did seem likely. Self-employment increased from 11.1% of all those in employment in 1984 to 13.4% in 1996 (Chart 9.1), especially among older men. Redundancies were accompanied by the buying back of some former employees' services, provided on a self-employed basis. Other workers used their savings to go independent.[2]

However, there has been no clear trend toward self-employment since the mid 1990s. Self-employment fell back from its 1996 level to 11.8% in 2001, before climbing again to 12.8% in 2004, which was still lower than in the mid 1990s. This stability of self-employment is not dissimilar to long-term trends in the United States, where the rate of full-time self-employment has held steady at about 8.5% a year for the last 40 years.[3]

---

[1] For example, Valerie Bayliss, *Redefining Work. An RSA Initiative*, London: RSA, 1998, p. 9.
[2] Self-employment among older men increased by about 50% between the mid 1980s and early 2000s. Richard Disney and Denise Hawkes, 'Why Has Employment Recently Risen Among Older Workers in Britain?' in Richard Dickens, Paul Gregg and Jonathan Wadsworth, *The Labour Market Under New Labour,* Basingstoke: Palgrave, 2003, pp. 56-7.
[3] Richard Sennett, *The Corrosion of Character,* New York: W. W. Norton, 1998, p. 141.

Chart 9.1 *The changing rate of self-employment (Self employed, UK, seasonally adjusted, total in 000's)*

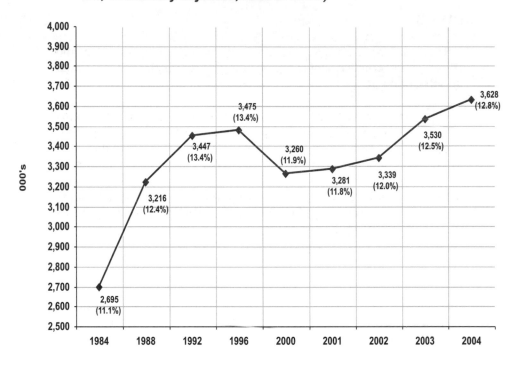

Source: ONS Labour Market Statistics, Integrated FR LFS TIME PERIODS, Table MGRQ.

What about people who have set up their own business and are employed by it, working on their own or with two or three other colleagues? A couple of friends might set up a company, for example. This might feel like self-employment, but is technically different.

Chart 9.2 shows that the number of people working in micro-companies (with one to four employees) increased significantly in the mid 1990s, but has remained pretty stable since. The number of people working for their own company but not employing anyone else ('enterprises with no employees'), a category that overlaps with self-employment, has also remained comparatively stable. In neither case has there been a trend toward patterns of work that approximate self-employment.

Chart 9.2 *Employment in UK enterprises with no employees and 1-4 employees 000s*

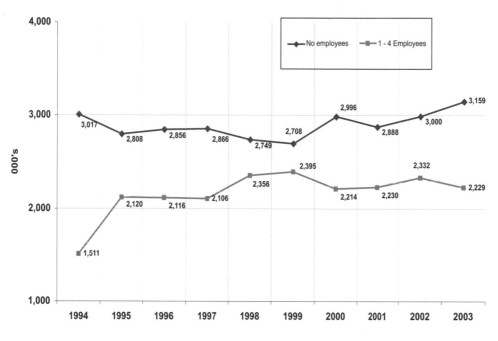

Source: Small Business Service.

The idea that we are headed toward self-employment or forms of work like it is not supported by recent trends. But might the picture change?

The next 20 years

The value attached to the personal will influence how many people work for themselves. Self-employment and micro-businesses are very much about personal identity – about finding meaning through your own creative activity rather than through consumption or your place on a career ladder. That is one reason why owner-managers are notoriously independent and often resist outside 'help' or 'interference', depending on your point of view.[4]

The great majority of micro-businesses also have a strong personal commitment to their customers. Whereas larger organisations seek to personalise their customer relationships through sophisticated research, tiny businesses have relationships with people, not computer models of people. Their offers are personal, not personalised.[5]

---

[4] Ted Fuller, 'If you wanted to know the future of small business what questions would you ask?', *Futures,* 35(4), 2003, p. 312.

[5] Ted Fuller, 'Communications for Small and Medium Enterprises in a Digital Age', 2002, http://tbs-home.tees.ac.uk/staff/U0019084/workingpapers/digital%20communications/CSMEDA.htm.

So how far society values the personal will help determine whether there is a culture friendly to self-employment and micro-firms. On the one hand, the trend toward personalisation reflects a reaction against the standardisation of mass consumption. Consumer markets will continue to fragment as individuals look for products that are just right for them. This should create openings for small enterprises built around the personal.

As prosperity has increased, consumer choice has widened and 'deference' has gone out of fashion, young people have come to expect more autonomy. They are better-educated and so perhaps more confident in exercising autonomy than their predecessors. Self-employment could be a natural outlet for individuals wanting greater control over their lives.

A Prince's Trust survey in 2000 found that two-fifths of 11 to 16 year olds had decided they were going to work for themselves. This was twice as high as five years earlier. In the same year, a record 80,000 aspiring entrepreneurs, up by 55% on 1999, approached Shell Livewire, which advises 20 year olds starting in business.[6] Were these 'flashes in the pan' or signs of an emerging trend?

On the other hand, the more that personal meanings are colonised by corporate symbols – 'I have status because I can buy this brand' – the less potential will exist for micro-enterprises. Consumers will be attracted to established brands instead of highly personal products. Individuals will seek identity in consumption rather than self-employment, and may value the security of employment to achieve their consumerist goals. What balance will be struck between the personal and the corporate?

The relative power of the corporate sector, it follows, will be an important driver. Independent entrepreneurs are part of the soil in which mega-companies flourish. Sometimes they are the suppliers and customers of a big firm. Occasionally they innovate on behalf of large companies: a small business may try a new idea, and if it works a corporate whale may swallow the firm up. But if the corporate sector has too much power, micro-businesses may be stifled.

The growth of personal services will create new opportunities for enterprising individuals. As prosperity rises, individuals will pioneer new forms of personal service such as organising house moves, offering IT support for people at home, advising on fitness and other activities that have emerged in recent years. Just over 70% of small businesses are in the services.[7]

More strategic outsourcing (see chapter 12) will create opportunities for individuals to supply advice and other services. The local management of schools, for instance, has encouraged individuals and micro-firms to provide training and other offerings to schools in competition with local authorities.

---

[6] *The Sunday Times,* 8 April 2001.
[7] *Annual Small Business Survey 2003. Executive Summary,* London: DTI, 2004, available on http://www.sbs.gov.uk/content/analytical/annualsbssummary.pdf.

But for how long will new initiatives flourish before the corporate sector takes them over? Chains of salons have transformed the hairdressing business, for example, sometimes squeezing out independent operators. Despite exceptions, 'independents' offering services on-line may struggle to compete with well-known brands, which will be more trusted.

As we discuss in chapter 12, some employers will 'in-source' key activities to secure more control, reducing the opportunities for tiny suppliers. Tight labour markets will encourage others to make permanent employment attractive. Some organisations will not want to depend on independent contractors, who might give preference to a competitor. Still others will control their suppliers so tightly that entrepreneurs may feel like workers without rights. 'Why bother?' they may ask.

Corporations will increasingly harness entrepreneurial talent for their own purposes. Budding entrepreneurs may be drawn into them if organisations increasingly generate knowledge that individuals find difficult to acquire on their own. Even more than today, generating knowledge will be a collective activity, and organisations may have greater ability to assemble people with relevant expertise than individuals.

Through corporate venturing, larger organisations may finance and support 'intrapreneurs' – in-company entrepreneurs.[8] More companies may franchise their operations to increase innovation, motivation among frontline staff and responsiveness to local conditions. Might some organisations decentralise so radically that workers end up with an autonomy that is closer to self-employment, but without the risks (see chapters 12 & 13)? Becoming an entrepreneur might be less attractive than being an 'intrapreneur'.

Will the space for independent operators contract rather than expand in the years ahead?

Electronic networks will increase connectivity and make it easier to specialise. If you are isolated, you have to do everything yourself. But when you are connected on-line, you can buy in back-office and other support, freeing you to maximise your expertise.[9] As electronic networks develop, they will extend the range of websites, blogs and other sources from which 'know-how' can be gathered.

Huge advances in communications will offer entrepreneurs planet-wide opportunities. Even now, someone in Cornwall can use the net to advertise across the globe – if a job offer comes from Brazil, they can decide whether it is worth moving for a few months. The expansion of 'knowledge' work will create occupations that can more readily be done from a distance, often by virtual teams

---

[8] Ted Fuller, 'If you wanted to know . . .' *op. cit.*, p. 316.
[9] Ibid, p. 314.

of legal, financial, marketing and other experts, assembled from around the world for specific tasks.

Young people who have grown up networking on-line may be more comfortable collaborating with others than some traditional entrepreneurs. A young adult with two businesses, for example, cooperated with a teenager who had four. All six enterprises were in virtual space. In their most recent venture, risk was shared with eight other partners.[10] Many young people are more IT 'savvy' than their elders, leaving them better placed to seize self-employment opportunities created by the knowledge economy.

But networks can be a mixed blessing. When they are open, they more easily assimilate budding entrepreneurs: when they are closed, they exclude outsiders and make it harder for novices to enter the field. On-line networks have the potential to be more open than face-to-face ones. Yet typically on-line and face-to-face go together.[11] Firms in a sector still cluster because they value the advantages of physical proximity, even though they talk to each other by email.

This need for physical presence will offset some of the advantages of open electronic networks. As now, potential entrepreneurs may fail to get started because they live too far away or don't know the right people to access physically the contacts they need.

The search for stability may discourage people from going independent. Many individuals now have 'liquid lives', with a plethora of choices from what to buy, to what values to identify with, to what living arrangements to make with their partner, to what school to choose for their children, to whether they should retire abroad.

Most choices carry a degree of risk – 'Is this the best choice?' 'What will happen if I get it wrong?' 'If I make this choice, what alternative will I have to forego – and might it be better?' 'What will my friends think?' As rising affluence continues to multiply choice, the risks associated with choosing will grow too. Individuals will want safe options. Most will prefer employment to self-employment to avoid yet more risky decisions. Might the desire for stability trump the desire for autonomy?

---

[10] Ted Fuller, 'Communications for Small . . .' *op.cit.*
[11] Steve Woolgar, 'Five Rules of Virtuality' in Steve Woolgar (ed.), *Virtual Society?*, Oxford: OUP, 2002, pp. 16-19.

On the other hand, our faster, faster society will continue to generate a multiplicity of business opportunities. Larger companies will often be slower to seize them than micro-firms, leaving gaps in the market for individuals to exploit. The same turbulence that will encourage many people to seek the stability of employment will increase openings for the enterprising minority.

What might be the implications?

The individualisation of work may have been exaggerated. The common perception that individualised work will steadily replace the collectivist workplace rests on a three-legged assumption that self-employment and micro-businesses will expand, workers will move more rapidly from one employer to another, with little loyalty to any one, and trade unions will decline while individual rights at work are extended.

But the future strength of the first leg of this stool is by no means guaranteed. Will a more 'personal' culture favouring entrepreneurs emerge? Will the corporate sector leave more space for tiny businesses? Will new networking opportunities on-line be offset by the quest for stability and a stronger preference for employment?

Currently, there is no significant trend to self-employment and micro-companies. So might the future be more about communities of employees and how they change than about solo forms of employment – as now, more about organisations than about individuals on their own?

Increasing enterprise is a priority across the political spectrum. Sometimes this is seen as encouraging self-employment and new businesses. But the continued dominance of employment suggests that stimulating entrepreneurial activity within organisations rather than outside may be more effective. What measures would encourage employers to foster and release the innovative potential of their employees?

Improving skills is another generally shared goal. A future in which more people were self-employed would have required individuals to take responsibility for building work-related skills throughout their lives. This was one of the ideas behind the notion of 'employability', a key part of the labour market rhetoric in the 1990s.

Yet in a future where the vast majority of the workforce is employed, individuals will be reluctant to assume responsibility for training. Most will expect the employer to pay. Policy initiatives to develop skills, therefore, will continue to focus on employer-led forms of training. 'Individual learning accounts' and other initiatives to empower individuals to access continued learning may have a smaller part to play than the 1990s rhetoric implied.

Given the central role of employers, might more organisations broaden out their training agendas? Some corporate 'universities', for example, include subjects that are not strictly work-related. To secure an advantage in tight labour markets, might other employers widen the scope of their training provision? Might the future of life-long learning in its broadest sense lie, to a large extent, with employers?

Points to take away

• Self-employment or employment in micro-companies is unlikely to accelerate.

• The policy challenge will be to encourage more entrepreneurship within organisations.

10. Is the end of 'jobs for life' a myth?

• One job per person has stayed the norm, permanent full-time employment remains dominant, workers are not moving more often from one employer to another and the 'career' – as a way of viewing work – has triumphed. The content of jobs has changed more than their duration.

• Workers will want stable employment for financial reasons, while employers will want the same to aid the accumulation of knowledge, hang on to key staff and manage change more easily.

• The 'contingent' workforce is unlikely to grow at the expense of permanent employment. Change will continue to occur more in job content than in the frequency of movement between jobs.

Central to the new folklore about work in the 1980s and 90s was that 'jobs for life' had come to an end. Work was being reshaped around the individual, who would move frequently from job to job and often hold more than one job as 'portfolio' working took off.

The story so far

The end of 'jobs for life' has become so deeply ingrained in our culture that few question it. But evidence to support the claim is fragile.

One job per person has stayed the norm. In 2000, 96% of workers had one job, a far cry from the portfolio working much vaunted in the late 80s and 1990s.[1] Instead of individuals performing two or more tasks for different organisations, there is more 'portfolio' working within organisations, as individuals switch from task to task for the same employer.

Permanent, full-time employment is still dominant. According to a large, representative survey of households across Britain, 94.1% of working men and 91.6% of women were in permanent jobs at the turn of the century. 95.2% of men and 73.3% of women worked full-time. (Table 10A)

Table 10A Proportion (%) of workers in different types of employment, by gender, at the turn of the century.*

Contract	Men	Women
Permanent	94.1	91.6
Seasonal/casual	2.2	3.3
Fixed-term contract	2.0	2.7
Agency temping	1.7	2.5

---

[1] *Employment Now – 1 million more people in work*, London: DfEE, 2000, p. 17.

Employment status
Part-time	4.8	26.7
Full-time	95.2	73.3

Source: British Household Panel Survey. Figures cited by Alison L. Booth & Jeff Frank, 'Gender and Work-Life Flexibility in the Labour Market' in Diane M. Houston (ed.), Work-Life Balance in the 21st Century, Basingstoke: Palgrave, 2005, p. 14.

*Figures for 'Contract' are from the 1999 and 2000 waves of the survey, while figures for 'Employment status' were calculated from 1991 to 2000 waves.

The Labour Force Survey shows that the proportion of people working in non-permanent employment has remained fairly constant (see Chart 10.1). Temporary employment peaked in 1997 with eight per cent of the population reporting temporary contracts. The proportion then declined to six per cent in 2003, the same as ten years earlier.[2]

Chart 10.1 The percentage of people working in non-permanent jobs, 1993 and 2003

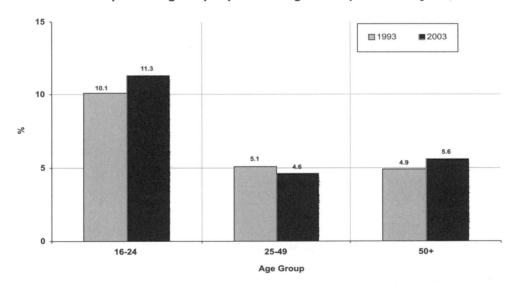

Source: Trish McOrmond, 'Changes in working trends over the past decade', Labour Market Trends, 112(1), 2004, p. 31.

Of those doing temporary work in 2003, four per cent were in seasonal work, down from six per cent in 1993; 19% were doing casual work, down from 22%; and just under half were on fixed contracts, roughly the same as 10 years earlier. The only category showing an increase was agency work, up from 7% to 18%.[3]

---

[2] Trish McOrmond, 'Changes in working trends over the past decade', *Labour Market Trends,* 112(1), 2004, p. 31.

[3] Ibid, p. 31.

But some forms of agency work have become more like permanent employment. Manpower, the largest employment agency, is the direct employer of its employees and seeks to develop a permanent relationship with at least some of them. Large, multinational agencies have gone beyond the traditional supply of 'temporary help' to provide an entire labour function, such as staffing a call centre and providing managers to supervise the 'insourced' workforce on site.[4]

Employment remains comparatively stable. In the 1992 Britain at Work Survey, only about a quarter of employees below the management/professional level thought their best chances lay in staying with their present employer; more than twice as many thought they would be best served by moving. Eight years later the position was reversed. In the 2000 Working in Britain Survey, most lower-level employees saw their best chances in staying, not moving.[5] The desire for stability of employment had increased.

This was reflected in people's behaviour. Over the same period, the time individuals spent with one employer did not fall, as many suppose, but actually increased. It went up from an average of six years and two months to seven years and four months.[6]

Other studies have reached similar conclusions. Labour Force Survey data for 1975 to 2000, for example, shows considerable variation between groups – 'job tenure' for women with dependent children increased, but fell for men and women without dependent children, especially men over 50. Overall, there was no clear trend for workers to move more frequently from one employer to another.[7]

This is similar to across the Atlantic. 'On average, tenure with a firm in the United States has been relatively constant, falling a bit for less educated young men and rising for women. Most employees still seek long-term jobs, and many temporary workers and agencies operate in part as a means for training and testing future permanent workers.'[8]

---

[4] Edmund Heery, Hazel Conley, Rick Delbridge & Paul Stewart, 'Beyond Enterprise? Trade Unions and the Representation of Contingent Workers', *Future of Work Series – Working Paper 7*, Leeds: ESRC Future of Work Programme, n.d., pp. 5-6, 16.

[5] Michael White, Stephen Hill, Colin Mills and Deborah Smeaton, *Managing to Change?*, Basingstoke: Palgrave Macmillan, 2004, pp. 57-8.

[6] Peter Nolan & Stephen Wood, 'Mapping the future of work', *British Journal of Industrial Relations,* 41 (2), 2003, pp. 168-9.

[7] For a review of this and another similar study see Claire Macaulay, 'Job mobility and job tenure in the UK', *Labour Market Trends,* 111(11), 2003, p. 541-2. Contrary evidence, the theme of the article, comes from the New Earnings Survey Panel Dataset, which shows that the median time spent with an employer fell significantly between 1996 and 2001. But this may reflect an upswing in the economic cycle. The General Household Survey data suggests that job tenure tends to fall during an upswing and lengthens in a downturn.

[8] Richard B. Freeman, 'The World of Work in the New Millennium' in Richard N. Cooper & Richard Layard (eds), *What the Future Holds,* Cambridge, Massachusetts: MIT, 2003, p. 169.

The 'career' – as a way of viewing work – has triumphed. In the 2002 survey, managers in over three quarters of the largest establishments said their workplaces had well-defined career ladders or a sequence of jobs that all employees who performed well could climb. A 'strikingly high' proportion of employers sought to provide all their workers with a sense that their job should be seen as part of a career progression.[9]

Indeed, between 1985 and 2001, the proportion of employees seeing themselves as having a career jumped from just under half to over 60%. The biggest increase – from 14% to 34% - was among low-paid groups like bus and coach drivers, packers and cleaners.[10] Significantly for the future, young people appear firmly wedded to careers.[11]

The content of jobs has changed more than their duration. Perhaps the biggest change in the workplace has been in the nature of jobs that people do. These have altered rapidly, mainly due to ICT. By 2002 ICT had impacted every job, or something very close to that, in one in three workplaces. Only one in twenty workplaces had virtually no ICT.[12]

Alongside technological advance, the spread of multi-tasking, team work and other aspects of 'high performance' management have transformed the content of most jobs.[13] 'All change' has occurred within workplaces rather than taking the form of movement between workplaces.

The end of 'jobs for life' has become a widespread myth for several reasons.

> • It fitted the growing fluidity of people's lives within a culture of choice. Other aspects of life were becoming more flexible – not least organisations kept changing. So it was natural to assume that employment was becoming less stable too.

---

[9] Robert Taylor, *Managing Workplace Change,* ESRC Future of Work Programme Seminar Series, Swindon: ESRC, 2003, p. 12.

[10] Michael Rose, 'Career Perceptions and Career Pursuit in the UK, 1986-2002' in Paul Stewart (ed.), *Employment, Trade Union Renewal and Future of Work,* Basingstoke: Palgrave, 2004, pp. 253-61.

[11] A 2002 study of 50 twenty to thirty-four year olds in a wide range of jobs in Bristol found a high level of career orientation. Harriet Bradley, Ranji Devadason, Steve Fenton, Will Guy & Jackie West, 'Young Adults Experience of Work in the "New" Economy: Initial Themes from an Explorative Project in 2002' in Paul Stewart (ed.), *Employment, Trade Union Renewal and the Future of Work,* Basingstoke: Palgrave, 2004, pp. 271-83.

[12] Michael White, Stephen Hill, Colin Mills and Deborah Smeaton, *op. cit.,* p. 17.

[13] In their 2000 survey, two thirds of employees received training to carry out a range of different tasks according to need. More than a half said they worked in a group, up by 10% since 1992. Michael White, Stephen Hill, Colin Mills and Deborah Smeaton, *op. cit.,* pp. 41, 45.

• Many workers lost their jobs in the recessions of the early 1980s and early '90s. Employment felt insecure – a feeling that global competition has kept alive in some cases. It was easy to make the (illogical) leap that if some jobs were insecure now, all jobs were becoming insecure always.

• With more people staying on at school and going to university, late teenagers and early twenty somethings were not the only ones in and out of jobs, looking for their niche. Graduates in their mid twenties to early thirties were doing the same. Young people were finding their feet in the labour market at a later age. But this was mistaken for a new pattern of behaviour that would be typical of Generation X throughout their lives.

The next 20 years

Since the future need not be the same as the past, it is conceivable that rapid change at work and more flexible mindsets will shorten 'job tenures' in future. Might we be headed for 'no jobs for life', only the future was hailed too soon? This seems unlikely:

Employees will want stable employment for financial reasons. They will have mortgages to service, families to support and retirement to prepare for. Moving to a new employer can be risky – 'last in, first out'. The more stable jobs are, the harder it will be to find a vacancy elsewhere.

Workers may also want stable employment because it will simplify their lives. As every day living becomes more complex, the search will be on to keep life easy to manage. When both partners are employed, for example, having to move house because one of them has switched jobs can be a problem. The proportion of households that moved home because of jobs halved between 1984 and 1994, and has fallen again since.[14] People are looking for stability.

Stable employment will aid the accumulation of knowledge. A churn in knowledge workers would require employers to store knowledge and pass it on quickly to new arrivals, lest the organisation be stranded when a key person left.

Yet despite emerging methodologies, techniques for capturing 'soft' knowledge, such as what makes a supplier 'tick', are likely to evolve slowly and remain problematic. Codifying and storing tacit knowledge can be difficult when busy staff give it a low priority, for instance. For a while to come, employers will want to retain key workers to build up their knowledge base.

Likewise, heavier investment in training will favour stable employment. The 'knowledge' and 'service' economies will require employers to invest substantial sums in training, which a growing number have been doing.

---

[14] http://www.racfoundation.org/our_research/Commutepaper.htm, 14/9/2003.

In particular, increasing employees' customer-facing skills will be an ever higher priority as consumers become more demanding. With automation transforming their jobs, might supermarket checkout staff for instance be trained as shopping advisers, perhaps helping customers to select a healthy balance of foods?

Employers will not want to squander their investment in training by making it easy for workers to move elsewhere. So they will continue to develop packages that encourage employees to stay.

In some cases they may want to retain labour to ensure that training takes place. The spread of freelance labour in the television industry in the early 1990s contributed to a sharp drop in the skills base of the industry. Employers complained about skill shortages and said that training for freelancers was inadequate. Partly as a result, companies encouraged freelancers to return to permanent contracts.[15]

Organisations will want to hang on to key staff. Much of the private sector will experience intense global competition, while the public sector will face rising value-for-money expectations. Managers will remain under pressure to control costs at every point, including the costs of recruitment and induction. High labour turnover is expensive.

Negotiating contracts with freelance staff can be costly, too. In the early 1990s, 58% of employers surveyed in the TV industry complained that freelance employment imposed an extra administrative expense.[16] Keeping workers will keep down costs.

To retain key staff, employers will seek even a marginal advantage in labour markets where skills are tight. They will improve fringe benefits, enhance the overall employment experience and in some cases espouse values close to their employees' hearts. As organisations are beginning to recognise, brands will need to attract employees as well as consumers.

Managing change will be easier with a stable workforce. Organisations will be required constantly to improve their working practices. Long-serving managers will have high levels of tacit knowledge, such as knowing others in the organisation, which will smooth the change process. Low labour turnover will allow organisations to spend less on employing new staff and more on helping existing workers adapt. A stable workforce that keeps adopting new approaches will be less resistant to change - 'this is how we have always done it' will have new meaning.

---

[15] Peter Nolan & Gary Slater, 'The Labour Market: History, Structure and Prospects' in Paul Edwards, *Industrial Relations: Theory and Practice,* Oxford: Blackwell, 2003, pp. 69-70.

[16] Ibid, pp 69-70.

What might be the implications?

The 'contingent' workforce is most unlikely to grow at the expense of permanent employment. The open-ended, permanent contract appears set to remain the norm for most employees. The idea that the future lies with contingent work – transitory, non-permanent employment – has been much exaggerated. This bodes well for employee security, so long as the employing organisation is itself financially sound.

Change will occur more in the content of jobs than in the frequency of movement between jobs. Britain's so-called flexible labour market will increasingly be about doing jobs in more flexible ways, as we discuss in chapter 17, rather than moving from one organisation to another. Indeed, as we have seen, stable employment may be vital to improve methods of work.

Moving up the value chain and meeting competition will force organisations to adopt new technologies, which will continue to advance at an accelerating pace. Many of these technologies will transform work.

For example, medical graduates are beginning to use i-pods containing summaries of relevant research. I-pods can be plugged in to update the material. As time memorising information is spent on developing more sophisticated ways of using it, changes in the practice of medicine will become even faster. Other occupations are likely to follow suit.

Work will remain an important component of personal identity. The increase in people seeing their work as a career points in this direction. In a 2002 survey of young adults in Bristol, a twenty-six year old shop assistant spoke for a number in the sample when she said, 'Work is my only main priority.'[17]

Fairly stable employment will reinforce this identification with work. If you remain a long time in a career, it will be natural as now for you to define yourself partly in terms of that career - 'I'm a researcher'. Staying with an employer will also encourage you to identify with a specific organisation.

The idea that identity will be predominantly about lifestyle – what you buy as a consumer – is almost certainly an exaggeration. Among the many components of identity, work will remain extremely important. Sir Clive Woodward, coach of the 2005 British Lions rugby tour to New Zealand, remarked in an interview, 'The work-life balance is crap. If you're lucky, work is a fundamental part of your life…Work is always with me because I love it.'[18]

---

[17] Harriet Bradley, Ranji Devadason, Steve Fenton, Will Guy & Jackie West, *op, cit.,* p. 277.
[18] *The Daily Telegraph,* 16 April, 2005.

But in what ways will people identify with work? Employment often exposes the individual to competing values and expectations. In the public services, for example, workers can be caught between a traditional public service ethos and the new managerialism, with its emphasis on targets, value for money and transparency. They can choose to identify with one or the other. Their choice shapes how they see themselves.[19]

As change accelerates and the workplace becomes more diverse and complex, the number of 'values streams' may increase. Work identities will be based not just on your occupation, but on how you see your job within that occupation - 'do I identify with the new approach of management, or with groups that are resisting?'

This will add another layer of complexity to lives that will already be complicated. Will the demand grow for help in managing these complexities?

Points to take away

• Long-term, full-time jobs will be far more typical for adults in the prime of life than portfolio working and temporary employment.

• Employers who invest in knowledge workers will develop employment strategies that enable them to keep their staff.

---

[19] For examples of how varied and complex this process can be, see Annette Davies and Robyn Thomas, 'Changing Professional Identities under New Public Management: A Gendered Perspective' in in Paul Stewart (ed.), *Employment, Trade Union Renewal and Future of Work,* Basingstoke: Palgrave, 2004, pp. 64-86.

11. Will home-working take off?

• There has been a steady progression to more mobile forms of work.

• Working mainly from home is likely to expand in remoter parts of Britain. Working from home for some of the time will continue to spread mainly among managerial and professional staff. Mobile work will remain the most important growth category.

• For many people, work and leisure will be less distinct, managing time will be a key issue, new forms of management control will be developed and more workers will have greater discretion over when they travel, perhaps helping to even out the commuter rush to some extent.

Another part of the 1980s and '90s folklore about work was that more and more people would work from home. Chief executives would say privately that home working was the future, and then announce a spanking new office! By the end of the nineties it was obvious that people would not swap work in the office for work at home: they would do both. The conventional wisdom now is that growing numbers will work from home for just part of the week.

But this is too static. The big picture is not about combining work in the office with work at home. It is about individuals moving from a few to many workplaces. Not everyone will be affected of course, but a substantial minority will. For a substantial proportion of workers, work in 20 years time will be more about movement than staying put.

The story so far

There has been a steady progression to more mobile forms of work over the past 20 years.

First, 'open plan' replaced the privacy of the small office with shared, dedicated spaces for individual employees. Most medium-sized and larger workplaces now use open plan. In the 2002 survey, nearly three in ten workplaces (28%) said they had been increasing their use of open plan, and one in five planned to use it more in the coming year.[1] As manufacturing has declined, services employment has come to look more like a factory.

---

[1] Michael White, Stephen Hill, Colin Mills & Deborah Smeaton, *Managing to Change?*, Basingstoke: Palgrave, 2004, p. 73.

Secondly, in the late 1980s and 90s 'hot-desking' began to replace dedicated spaces with shared spaces. Instead of individuals having their own desks and areas in open plan, certain desks are used by anyone on an 'as needed' basis.

In 2002 hot-desking was being used at one in four workplaces. This included one in seven workplaces with five to 24 employees, small enough for the whole operation to be run in this way, and three in ten workplaces with 100 or more employees (but where only part of the organisation might be affected). One in eight workplaces planned to introduce hot-desking, or extend its use, in the coming year.[2]

Thirdly, space at home, in the hotel, on trains and in planes has begun to rival space in the office. According to the Labour Force Survey, in 1981 around one in 25 of the labour force (4.3%) worked mostly at or from home: by 2002 this had more than doubled to exactly one in 10, accounting for 2.8 million people.

By far the greatest increase was in people 'working mainly in different places, using home as a base', which tripled from 2.8% to 7.6%. Those 'working mainly in own home', by contrast, went up more slowly, from 1.5% in 1981 to 2.7% ten years later, before falling back to 2.4% in 2002.

A third category, people 'working mainly elsewhere [from the office] but also at least one full day at or from home', accounted for 4.0% of the labour force in 1997, slightly over a million people. These figures had leapt to 4.4% and 1.2 million by 2002.

If we pull these three categories together, in 2002 almost 3.8 million people (13.4%) worked either mainly in their own home, or mainly in different places using home as a base, or mainly elsewhere but also one full day at home. This was a startling jump on the near 3 million (11.3%) who were working in these ways a mere five years earlier. What has increased is not so much homeworking, as people working in multiple centres. The conventional workplace as a centre for employment is being chipped away.[3]

Might this be the tip of an iceberg? The three categories just referred to all include a significant element of home-based working. Estimates based on the 2002 Change in Employer Practices Survey suggests that 14.3% employees worked most of the time off-site with customers or clients, and a further 3.5% spent some of their usual hours working from home. On this basis, approaching a fifth of all employees were working away from their employer's premises for at least part of the week.

---

[2] Michael White, Stephen Hill, Colin Mills & Deborah Smeaton, *op. cit.,* p 75.
[3] Alan Felstead, Nick Jewson & Sally Walters, *The Changing Place of Work*, Working Paper 28, ESRC Future of Work Programme, n.d., Table 1.

The large number working off-site with customers or clients indicates that the trend is not toward homeworking per se, but to more mobile forms of work. Workers are on the move. The trend was set to continue. 13.5% of surveyed managers expected more of their employees to be working off-site with customers or clients in the coming year.[4]

The next 20 years

Working mainly from home is likely to expand in remoter parts of Britain. Working from home for some of the time will continue to spread mainly among managerial and professional staff. Mobile work will remain the most important growth category.

Full-time home-working

Substantial improvements in IT will enable full-time home-working. Video-conferencing at home will become commonplace in the next decade, for example. The demand will come from the significant number of people who are likely to leave the cities for a home in the countryside – possibly around four million over the next 20 years, on top of the 14 million who now live in predominantly rural areas.[5] In parts of Devon and Cornwall in the early 2000s, as many as 18-20% of the population worked from home, over twice the national average.[6]

But there will be limits to how far this pattern will spread. Many jobs do not lend themselves to being done mainly at home, such as jobs requiring specialist equipment, meetings with colleagues or face-to-face contact with the customer. When you add these up – health professionals, teachers, waiters, shelf-stackers, taxi drivers, electricians, carers and many others – the numbers are considerable.[7] Working mainly at home will remain a niche.

---

[4] Alan Felstead, Nick Jewson & Sally Walters, *op. cit.,* Table 9.

[5] Michael Moynagh & Richard Worsley, *The state of the countryside, 2020: Scenarios for the future of rural England,* Report to the Countryside Agency, 2003, p. 33.

[6] http://www.racfoundation.org/our_research/Commutepaper.htm, 14/9/2003. Figures are based on the Labour Force Survey.

[7] Some of these may eventually be capable of being done remotely, of course, but it is unclear how far patients – for example – will be satisfied with a consultation at a distance.

Part-time home-working

Part-time home-working will continue to grow significantly, but will hit some of the same constraints that will limit the expansion of full-time work at home. Growth will be most marked among managerial, professional and associate professional staff, who comprised 57.7% of those who worked at least one day a week at or from home in 2000.[8]

Technology will be a great help to them. Between 1997 and 2002 the number of people whose home location of work depended on IT soared by 80.2%. 'This provides some empirical evidence for the ability of technology, via the electronic envelope, to stretch the reach of the conventional workplace well beyond the physical boundaries.'[9]

Working at home will help employees organise their work more effectively. Increasingly, individuals will divide their work between what needs to be done on their own without interruption, and what requires interaction with others. Working at home one or two days a week may also help parents to juggle the needs of children with the demands of the job.

Employers may also be able to push up individuals' volume of work. Commuting time can be spent working instead. The trade-off for more flexibility over when you work may be a willingness to do more work. 'Blackberrying' has encouraged some executives to deal with their emails on Sunday evenings to get a 'head start' on Mondays.

Reducing office space will remain an important driver. The cost of office space looms large within overheads, especially in expensive cities like London. In the late '90s and early 2000s, city centre commercial rates were rising at twice or triple the rate of inflation each year.[10] Having a portion of the workforce out of the office at any one time will be a significant saving.

A 2002 'Location of Work Survey' of large organisations in Britain found that senior facilities/property managers cited the need to economise on property costs, along with promoting work flexibility, as the main factor behind the trend to greater working at home.[11]

---

[8] Alan Felstead, Nick Jewson & Sally Walters, *op. cit.,* p 14.

[9] Ibid, p 11.

[10] Michael White, Stephen Hill, Colin Mills & Deborah Smeaton, *op. cit.,* p. 69.

[11] Alan Felstead, Nick Jewson & Sally Walters, *op. cit.,* p. 21.

Mobile work

The expansion of mobile work is likely to remain the fastest growing form of off-site employment. It will overlap with full and part-time home-working, but will increasingly be recognised as a distinct category. Individuals will not necessarily see themselves as working from home. They could equally be working from the office. But they will be on the move from place to place, working at various times of the day, for much of the week.

Even now it is possible to work in a hotel, an airport lounge or motorway service station, in a train, plane or car, in a cottage in Wales, at a wedding reception in Australia or on a beach in the Caribbean. You can work morning, noon or night, during the week or at weekends. You can be visiting suppliers, wooing customers or interviewing a job applicant in a hotel lounge. This mobile, fluid work will continue to spread.[12]

Technology will be an enabler. Already faxes, mobile phones, portable computers and dispersed terminals have enabled more people to work on the move. In future video phones, ubiquitous video conferencing (presumably available in hotels), Wi-Max (a more powerful variant of Wi-Fi) and perhaps holographic phones by the mid 2020s will dramatically improve the quality of individuals' connectedness. They will make it easier to stretch the workplace to any location the employee happens to be in.

The relational nature of work will be the key driver. We saw in chapter 2 how interpersonal relationships are becoming an ever more central component of work. Workers are spending more time interacting with customers, suppliers and others in their team.

Further advances in technology, such as far more powerful computer chips, will take automation to new extremes. Automation will encourage organisations to develop new products and improve existing ones. This will demand more meetings, more banging of heads together and more teams. At the same time, automation will make more complex tasks possible, requiring a more diverse range of skills. Workers will be forced to collaborate even more than they do today.

Much of this collaboration already occurs on-line. For a growing number of employees, work is increasingly about being immersed in the electronic transfer of messages and information. It is about flows of communication rather than the static processing of forms. This will be still more the case in future as the interpersonal dimension of work grows.

---

[12] It is well described by Alan Felstead, Nick Jewson & Sally Walters, *Changing Places of Work*, Basingstoke: Palgrave, 2005, forthcoming, which has informed this chapter.

As work becomes primarily about communication – a phone call here, a photo message there, a video conference somewhere else and emails everywhere – a larger slice of the workforce will not need to be in the office to do it. Individuals will be able to work any time, anywhere.

Often they will have to be on the move. Although electronic communications can sustain a relationship, frequently they are no substitute for face-to-face contact. Trust is created when people meet each other and talk outside the formal context – in the elevator, by the coffee machine or while they wait for the meeting to start. They begin to see each 'in the round' and get to know one another. By making collaboration across distances easier, e-communications will create more need for workers to meet each other – and to travel to do so.

So as relationships become more central to work, and as organisations separated by distance increasingly collaborate, mobile work will continue to spread. The future will not be mainly about the growth of home-working, but the expansion of mobile work.

The enduring office

But mobile work and home-working will not replace the office. The conventional workplace will retain its advantages. As now, it will enable organisations to pass on tacit knowledge ('the way we do things round here'), help managers to keep an eye on their staff, foster good relationships between workers (chit-chatting in the corridor for example), and encourage creativity and innovation through informal contacts. Firms often cluster near others in a similar business, which underscores the importance of 'physical presence' in many jobs.

From the individual's standpoint, the office will continue to provide a chance to make friends, enjoy the camaraderie of colleagues and catch up on the gossip – not to mention actually doing the job by collaborating with colleagues. Of 684 Institute of Management members who replied to a 1999 survey, only 16% said they would want to work from home full-time.[13]

The conventional workplace will far from disappear. But for many employees, it will become one of several locations for work. We are moving from workplace to work places.

---

[13] Michael Moynagh & Richard Worsley, *Tomorrow,* London: Lexicon, 2000, p. 29.

What might be the implications?

The spheres of work and leisure will become less distinct, as a result of these developments. Throughout most of the twentieth century, work and 'life' were clearly separate. Where and when you worked differed from the where and when of leisure. But for those involved, mobile work will blow these distinctions apart. A place and time will no longer be ring-fenced for work.

For many employees, three types of work spaces will predominate.[14]

- 'Working in collective offices' will involve, as increasingly now, space that is no longer allocated on an individual basis, but is shared with others, such as 'hot desks' and 'touchdown areas'.

- 'Working at home' will entail close physical proximity to the individual's domestic world and geographical distance from colleagues, co-workers and managers.

- 'Working on the move' will continue to comprise occupational tasks conducted while in transit from one location to another, sometimes at temporary stop-off points en route. Work will be conducted in impersonal arenas at some distance from colleagues and managers.

Mobile work and home-working will involve a shift from personalised space to personalised time. In the traditional office you had a room, or a desk with surrounding area in an open plan setting. These cubes of space belonged to the individual in that they were not available to others. Often workers personalised their space with pictures, plants and photographs.

As more people work on the move or at home for part of the time, these personal spaces will be replaced by the 'collective office', with hot-desking arrangements. Many employees will lose their personal space at work. Some will work in a highly personalised environment at home, but often this will not be entirely their space. It will be shared with the rest of the household. Others will be mobile, working in public rather than private spaces.

Offsetting this loss of personalised space will be the personalisation of time. Instead of fixed hours when they have to be at work, employees at home or on the move will have greater choice over when they work – late at night in the hotel, perhaps. Individuals will lose control over 'their' space, but get more control over their time.

---

[14] Alan Felstead, Nick Jewson & Sally Walters, *Changing Places of Work*, op. cit., ch 1.

Managing time will become an issue for this minority – but growing – section of the workforce. Once work weaves into all the nooks and crannies of your life, deciding when to work and when to shop, for instance, will be increasingly difficult. Getting the job done will compete with the family. Time with friends may be interrupted by calls from workmates. Managing time will add to life's complexity and become an extra source of family conflict.

Work may colonise idle time at home. Waiting to collect the children from swimming? I'll send my manager a message. The job will intrude on moments of personal reflection. Whatever the statutory limit on working hours, fluid time will help work to burrow into more of your time. Work will loom larger in individuals' lives. The work-life balance will be even harder to manage. What would help individuals to keep work in its proper place?

New forms of management control will be likely. In the traditional workplace, employees had fixed places that managers could watch. They had to be present at fixed times so that supervisors could keep an eye on them. Allocated places and allocated times were important instruments of management control.

As the time and place of work become more fluid Peter Thomson, director of the Future Work Forum at the Henley Management Centre, believes that managers will be forced to adopt new approaches to running the workplace.[15]

Some managers of mobile workers are trying to exercise control by adapting existing approaches. For example, they are extending surveillance through electronic means, such as requiring remote staff to keep electronic records of their work. Others are rethinking procedures to assert their authority through new methods like output management. Instead of measuring input – how much effort is the person devoting to the task? – they are measuring the results.

A number are seeking to be more radical. Instead of developing discrete techniques for regulating specific pieces of work ('this is how we'll measure your performance'), they are attempting to manage the fluidity of work as a whole. Their focus is on capturing workers' hearts and minds – not forcing them to do managers' will, but creating a culture in which employees want to achieve their managers' objectives.

Might fostering a collective identity and encouraging workers to ally themselves with the organisation be the means by which most managers – in the long run – gain control over their mobile workers?[16]

---

[15] Quoted in *The Times,* 28 May 2005.
[16] Alan Felstead, Nick Jewson & Sally Walters, op. cit.,

The expansion of mobile work and home-working could have a significant impact on the built environment. Individuals who use their home as a base, if only part-time, may seek larger homes. If they cannot afford the extra room, existing rooms will be redesigned. As is starting to happen, sitting rooms, bedrooms and kitchens will be purpose built to double up as an office.

Freed from the daily commute, more people will be able to live further from their employer's premises. They will have more choice of where to live. This will add to pressure on popular locations with a prestigious address, or which are near good schools and amenities. Property prices will diverge more widely, increasing the physical separation between rich and poor people. Mobile work will encourage migration to parts of the countryside within reach of communication hubs.

An increase in mobile work will encourage more people to travel. But this will not be entirely bad news for Britain's congested roads, rails and airports. Some work journeys will be alternatives to commuting. Others will take in visits, perhaps to the supermarket, that would have required a separate journey. Most important, workers will have more choice over when they travel. They won't have to join the commuter rush.

This may reinforce the case for road charges based on the density of traffic. (Government is currently examining the feasibility of a nationwide scheme, using satellite technology.) If more workers can decide when they travel, charges would be more effective in persuading people to travel at less congested times. Evening out the traffic peaks would enable roads to take more cars.

Points to take away

• The expansion of specifically home-working will be eclipsed by the continued expansion of mobile work – people who travel as part of their job.

• New techniques will be developed to manage mobile workers. Will these techniques help to transform the management of other employees?

12. How will organisations change?

> • Automation has re-engineered processes, boundaries have been blurred within organisations, collaborative networks have spread, dis-aggregation and re-aggregation have become commonplace, but the elimination of hierarchies may have reached a limit.
>
> • Competition, changing transaction costs, more sophisticated customisation, controlling risks and the capacity of management will influence the future of shape of organisations.
>
> • Some of today's forms of organisation will remain, alongside many new ones. Outsourcing will be more limited than many expect. Decentralisation will spread, but vertical organisations will still exist.

Much of the tumultuous change at work over the past 25 years has been associated with reorganisation. Organisations have closed, merged, bought up rivals, forged alliances, outsourced and restructured, often at bewildering speed. Change has been occurring around the workplace, as much as within it.

In 2003 almost 37% of UK employees worked in organisations employing 500 or more people, and nearly 54% were in organisations with 50 or more.[1] What will these organisations look like in 20 years' time? Will they be smaller and flatter, with many more operations outsourced? Or might changes take a different tack – and surprise us?

The story so far [2]

Automation has re-engineered processes. Robotics and IT in the motor and other industries have expanded customisation. Automating the movement as well as the production of watches has revolutionised the Swiss watch industry. Retail banking has been transformed by cash machines and on-line facilities. Secretarial jobs look very different thanks to the PC and email. Automation means that job after job is not what it used to be.

---

[1] Small Business Service.

[2] This section has been informed in particular by Prabhu Guptara, 'Managers' Lives, Work and Careers in the 21st Century' in Cary L. Cooper (ed.), *Leadership and Management in the 21st Century*, Oxford: OUP, 2004, pp. 107-38.

In the 2002 survey, one in three workplaces reported that virtually all their employees used computerised equipment in their jobs. Fully wired workplaces were evenly spread across small, medium and large enterprises. Only one in five workplaces was almost without IT.[3]

The blurring of boundaries has occurred within organisations. Bridges have been built between processes and departments that had had little to do with each other. Traditionally, for example, marketing had few links with R & D. Today that would be almost unthinkable. These new links have led to more advanced forms of customisation and cut the cycle time from ideas to 'product on the shelves' (often dramatically), contributing to a 'faster, faster' world.

Geographical boundaries in many companies have diminished. Only the most basic industries, such as building materials, are still organised by geographical division. In financial services, not one major company is organised on a geographical basis. Foreign exchange dealers trade with each other across the world, scarcely knowing the bonds dealer one floor below.

Walls between industries have been tumbling down. Sainsbury's and Marks and Spencer are just two retailers that have moved into financial services. Different products are increasingly bundled together, such as an airline ticket that comes with insurance, hotel booking, car hire, a guide book and a theatre ticket in the city of destination.[4]

Collaborative networks have become commonplace. They range from ad hoc teams within a department, to cross-departmental teams, to company-wide teams spanning the globe, to professional and other networks that jump organisations, to international supply chains, to collaborative ventures. The 2002 survey found that formally designated teams were on the increase in one in three workplaces.[5] But these were just the tip of the iceberg. Numerous informal networks also exist.

The dis-aggregation and re-aggregation of organisations has proceeded apace. Companies have outsourced and offshored like never before. More than nine in ten of the 2000 workplaces surveyed in 2002 had outsourced at least one type of activity. One half had outsourced four or more services, and nearly a fifth had recently outsourced work previously done by their own employees.[6]

The most usual types of outsourcing were in low-skilled activities like cleaning, catering and security. But employers were starting to outsource higher-skilled services, such as training (43%), ICT (26%) and recruitment (20%). BP is one

---

[3] Michael White, Stephen Hill, Colin Mills & Deborah Smeaton, *Managing to Change?*, Basingstoke: Palgrave Macmillan, 2004, p. 17.

[4] However, other parts of the travel industry are unbundling, such as package holidays as more people seek the flexibility of pick-'n-mix arrangements.

[5] Michael White, Stephen Hill, Colin Mills & Deborah Smeaton, *op. cit.,* p. 45.

[6] Ibid, pp. 25-6.

blue-chip employer that has outsourced much of its Human Resource Management function.[7]

Offshoring has become an important dimension of outsourcing. By 2004 perhaps around 6% of the UK's call centre jobs had gone abroad, rather lower than media comment might suggest, but a significant trend even so.[8]

The elimination of management layers seems to have reached a limit. As global competition intensified in the 1980s and early 90s, many companies de-layered to cut costs. But this flattening of hierarchies has been reversed somewhat at the turn of the century. To an extent, hierarchies and career ladders are back.

Twenty-two per cent of the managers in the 2002 survey said that the proportion of managerial and professional staff had risen in the previous three years, against 8% who thought there had been a decline and 69% who reported little change. [9] (See Chart 12.1)

Chart 12.1 *The number of managers has increased*

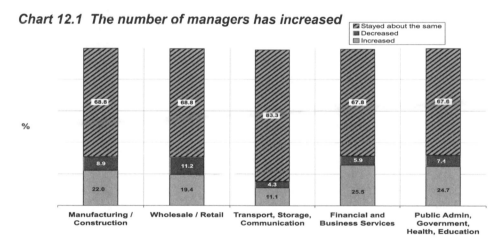

Source: Robert Taylor, *Managing Workplace Change,* Swindon, ESRC Future of Work Programme Seminar Series, p. 9

The same survey found that one in three workplaces was reshaping its grade structure over the same period. It is true that one in ten was slimming down their management grades and one in 14 was taking out grades below management level. But increases in the number of grades outweighed reductions by more than two to one (see Chart 12.2). 'It seems that the move toward flatter organisations and broader grades, which was evident in the late 1980s and early 1990s, has been short-lived.'[10]

---

[7] Michael White, Stephen Hill, Colin Mills & Deborah Smeaton, *op. cit.,* p. 26.
[8] Based on Datamonitor figures provided by CM Insight Ltd.
[9] Michael White, Stephen Hill, Colin Mills & Deborah Smeaton, *op. cit.,* p. 61.
[10] Ibid, p. 61.

Chart 12.2 *Workplaces increasing grades outnumber those which are decreasing*

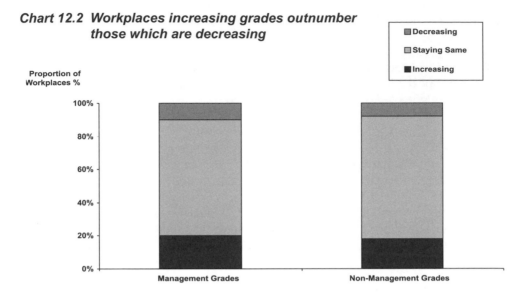

Source: Michael White, Stephen Hill, Colin Mills and Deborah Smeaton, *Managing to Change?* Basingstoke: Palgrave, 2004, p. 61.

The next 20 years

Many of these trends will continue. But what will they mean for the size of organisations, how many activities will be outsourced, the extent to which organisations will decentralise and how flat their management structures will be? Answers will depend on whether the dynamics behind recent trends will change in the future.

Competition, including user pressure to improve public service, will propel further organisational change. Companies will continue to consolidate to reduce competition. As in the past quarter century, take-overs, mergers, alliances and collaborative ventures will reshape entire sectors.

Fund managers, under competitive pressure themselves,[11] will demand greater transparency to assess firms' potential profitability. They will expect companies to be more rigorous in explaining themselves – 'This is our core business, these are our core competences, and this is the strategy to develop the business and defend our strengths.' Methodologies for defining, demonstrating and developing unique strengths will become more sophisticated.

---

[11] This will include not only competitive pressures, but as is already happening government demands that fund managers be more active in company affairs. Reflecting a trend Richard Saunders, chief executive of Investment Management Association (IMA), the trade body for the fund management industry, announced in March 2003 that the IMA planned to jolt the industry into greater focus on companies' wider strategy, as well as directors' pay. 'Fund managers vow to become more active shareholders', *The Times,* 14 March 2003.

Improving business processes will yield information on the strengths and weaknesses of each part of the operation, sometimes sparking further reorganisation. The introduction of team-based cellular working in the aerospace industry, for example, enabled managers to identify less profitable units for outsourcing.[12]

Competition will promote change, while technology will make change possible. Thirty per cent of the top 50 UK companies between 1992 and 2000 were engaged in large-scale reorganisation every year by the end of the decade, against 20% at the beginning.[13] As 'this is how we have always done it' becomes even more passé, the pace of change will accelerate further. An expectation of change will make it easier to innovate, which will make change still more rapid.

Senior managers will have even less time to process all the information and ideas filtering up from their juniors. They will be forced to empower local staff to cut the costs of moving information up and down the hierarchy, allow organisations to respond more quickly to changes in the local environment and encourage innovation. As discussed in the next chapter, organisations will delegate more and more decisions to teams, business units and individuals.

Companies will act more like a market than a socialist state.[14] For example, NHS foundation hospitals are said to be considering turning themselves into a collection of branded medical boutiques, on a Debenham's model. Each 'boutique' would operate under a concession from the top institutions with the best reputation for a particular speciality. Local hospitals would become customer service units, organising each patient's pathway through the boutiques.[15]

Changing transaction costs will reshape many organisations. Traditionally researching products, finding suppliers, negotiating contracts, monitoring performance and enforcing contracts were most efficiently overseen by a small, senior group that could hold the relevant information and use it to balance competing priorities. This has often favoured large organisations, in which a central team welded different units into a whole. 'Command and control' was more efficient than negotiating with each unit.

---

[12] Andy Danford, Mike Richardson, Paul Stewart, Stephanie Tailby & Martin Upchurch, 'High Performance Work Systems, Labour Control and the Production Worker' in Paul Stewart (ed.), *Employment, Trade Union Renewal and the Future of Work,* Basingstoke: Palgrave, 2005, p. 198.

[13] Richard Wittington and Michael Mayer, *Organising for Success in the Twenty-First Century,* London: CIPD, 2002, pp. 2-3.

[14] Gary Hamel & Liisa Valikangas, 'The Quest for Resilience', *Harvard Business Review,* Sept. 2003, p. 61.

[15] *Society Guardian,* 11 May 2005.

New technologies are making it easier to decentralise. Information can be held on vast databases, with access by many users. Video-conferencing and other electronic communication can bring diverse decision-makers together. Outsourced supply chains can be managed online. Priorities are beginning to be determined electronically according to pre-determined rules. The transaction costs of keeping in touch with units around the world have fallen dramatically. It has become much cheaper to decentralise.

These developments will continue to gather pace as information technology advances exponentially. For instance, the internet had daily peak traffic of 0.47 terabytes per second at the beginning of 2000 (a terabyte is one trillion bytes – groups of data bits which encode modules of information): by the end of 2001 this had leapt to 5.6 terabytes. 'The pace of growth in telecommunications volume in the period 1995-2000 implies that the entire information throughput of the year 2000 will be encompassed in one second in 2020.'[16] Transactions using broadband, mobile telephony and other technologies will see huge cost reductions.

But will lower transaction costs in one area be offset by higher costs in another? Delegation may slice the cost of passing information up and down the management chain, but ensuring that delegated decisions benefit the whole organisation can be extremely difficult and require considerable resources.

Giving business units greater discretion, negotiating rather than imposing targets on them and encouraging them to learn continuously will demand sophisticated knowledge management systems and high levels of expertise. Some organisations may find that the transaction costs of centralisation remain lower than for decentralisation – at least for a while.

More sophisticated customisation will require customer-facing staff to have greater discretion. Already hotel and other chains allow branches to do special deals. In future, individuals will not be content with customised products: as is starting to happen, they will expect the purchase transaction to be personalised too – 'don't treat me like another customer, treat me as an individual'.

Money will increasingly be made at the customer interface. The proliferation of mentors, personal trainers, lifestyle advisers, shopping advisers, style consultants and concierge services herald a trend in which today's often impersonal forms of customisation will give way to more personal approaches, in which 'choice managers' play a central role.[17]

---

[16] Oliver Sparrow, 'Telecommunications', 31/10/02, http://www.chforum.org/library/xc112.html.
[17] 'Choice manager' is Michael Willmott's helpful term in Michael Willmott, *Citizen Brands,* Chichester: Wiley, 2001, p. 159-60.

Self-service forms of customisation, where you go online and choose from a menu of options, will become the low-price option. High-value customers will not be bothered with online menus that take time and may not give them exactly what they want. They will want choice managers who, with minimal intrusion in the customer's life, can research the options, provide advice and produce tailor-made solutions.

Consumer expectations and greater affluence will drive the search for new forms of personalisation. Technology-induced savings elsewhere in the supply chain will make advanced personalisation affordable. The personal relationship between the customer and seller will emerge as a major – sometimes the major – source of value in the supply chain.[18]

Customer-facing organisations will dare not contract out this relationship, lest they lose a large source of revenue. Nor will they risk stifling locally designed customisation with too much central control. To establish a bespoke customer relationship, choice managers will not need a template: they will need the freedom to be responsive and creative (for which of course they will have to be trained). Decisions will be taken jointly with the customer rather than passed up the line.

Controlling risks will be another key influence on the shape of organisations. Delegating authority involves the delegation of risk. Staff acting in the name of the organisation may bring it into disrepute. One group may tread on the toes of another – a convenience store may stock a new line and take business from its parent's supermarket down the road. Tight financial controls cannot always be devolved.[19]

Central control enables top executives to use their knowledge and authority to prevent unnecessary risks. This will remain an important consideration. Competitive pressures, technology and customer relations may all encourage greater decentralisation, but senior managers will continue to ask, 'Dare we take the risk?'

The capacity of staff to manage change will be a fifth driver. As now, many organisations will be so pared to the bone that managers will scarcely have time to think strategically. Lack of management resources will delay and minimise change: managers will be too busy on other things. So, too, may the limited capacity of more junior staff to assume new responsibilities or work in new ways. Human failings will continue often to reduce the gains from reorganisation.

---

[18] This is discussed more fully by Shoshana Zuboff & James Maxmin, *The Support Economy*, London: Allen Lane, 2003.

[19] In the aerospace industry, for example, increased autonomy through the delegation of problem-solving responsibilities to teams has often been largely offset by tight management control of quality and costs. Andy Danford, Mike Richardson, Paul Stewart, Stephanie Tailby & Martin Upchurch, *op. cit.,* pp. 187-211.

What might be the implications?

So will organisations look very different in 20 years' time?

Variety will rule. Some of today's forms of organisation will remain, alongside many new ones. The following types of organisation are likely to spread, but doubtless there will be some surprises, too:[20]

- 'The virtual corporation' will rely on a network of market-based contracts to develop, manufacture, market, distribute and support its offerings. It will hardly be an organisation at all – more a network of contractors held together by legal bonds. It will be pioneered by entrepreneurs who can pull together a variety of skills to grasp an opportunity.

- 'The network organisation' will be semi-virtual, in that it will rely on external suppliers for many of its activities. But it will build more enduring, 'thicker' connections through joint venture agreements, formal alliances, interlocking shareholdings or longstanding contracts. It will tend to have a larger 'strategic centre', able to co-ordinate and direct the evolution of its activities.

- 'The boundary-less organisation' will use both external and internal networks. Relying on joint ventures and alliances, the boundaries between the organisation and its external partners will be highly porous. Information will flow freely across its 'borders' and people will work easily on either side. But there will also be a strong commitment to internal networks. Transnational corporations increasingly embody this approach.

- 'The project-based (or team) organisation' will assemble temporary groups of people according to the needs of each project. Sometimes the project or team will be the basis for the whole organisation, so that when the project is over the organisation dissolves too, as in the TV industry. More often these teams and projects will operate within a more stable organisational framework.

- 'The modular (or cellular) corporation' will comprise discrete units (or cells) that can be assembled into all sorts of combinations or simply transferred outside. Modules will be combined and recombined easily because they rely on common standards or procedures, such as unified information technology, consistent reward and career structures across the organisation, or uniform planning, investment appraisal or innovation processes.

---

[20] These categories are based on Richard Whittington & Michael Mayer, *op. cit.,* pp. 6-8.

• 'The process-based (or horizontal) organisation' will build on complete processes rather than traditional functional tasks. It will be the equivalent of a hierarchical organisation turned on its side. Managers will look across narrow departments along the horizontal track of meeting customer needs, rather than simply up and down according to traditional, vertical reporting lines.

Outsourcing will be limited. Some experts believe that the future is all about outsourcing – and that will certainly be true in some cases. Interviews with senior executives in the early 2000s found that the rationale for outsourcing activities abroad was changing. 'Companies are now going beyond mere cost savings and moving towards more radical business transformations such as foreign market entry and organisational restructuring.'[21] Offshoring – outsourcing to suppliers overseas – will continue to expand.

Not least, outsourcing could profoundly change parts of the public sector. Even now, the NHS is shifting more of its activities, such as hip operations, to specialist treatment centres. In time, the health service could be transformed into a brand managing body, commissioning services, ensuring quality and managing the NHS brand. Outsourcing specialists like LogicaCMG and Capita are wooing local and central government.

But other organisations will want to keep ownership of their activities, and even bring some back in-house. Several NHS hospitals have in-sourced cleaning to improve standards, for example. A recent article extolling the virtues of outsourcing conceded that – amazingly – only 10% of the top UK 100 companies had seriously begun the outsourcing process.[22] Outsourcing to suppliers in the UK may grow more slowly than many suppose.

The future will not be about outsourcing nor about in-sourcing, but a mixture of both. Combinations will vary from organisation to organisation and change over time. A business that has outsourced its HR functions may change its mind in the light of experience.

Competitive advantage will be the key consideration. Managers will become more adept at identifying their organisation's core strengths and developing an outsourcing strategy round them. If training gives you a unique advantage, you may want to keep that part of HR in-house and develop your expertise further.

Transaction costs will influence the decision. Will it be more time-consuming to negotiate with an outside supplier than to manage the process directly? Linked with this will be the question of control. 'If we outsource, will we have the same influence over quality, costs and delivery times? Might the supplier be tempted to give preference to a competitor?'

---

[21] Chris Odindo, Stephen Diacon & Christine Ennew, *Outsourcing in the UK Financial Services Industry: The Asian Offshore Market,* Financial Services Research Forum, Nottingham University Business School, 2004, p. 19.

[22] 'Focus Outsourcing', *The Times,* 25 January 2005. The 10% figure looks rather low.

When organisations do outsource, they may keep such tight control over their suppliers that the entire supply chain becomes rather like a single organisation, perhaps managed by a supply chain specialist. Other organisations may find it easier and cheaper to keep activities in-house. As far as individual workers are concerned, might both arrangements feel similar?

Decentralisation will spread – slowly, enabling units to become more nimble, innovative, responsive to market conditions and so more competitive. Technology will make this possible by reducing transaction costs, while the growing importance of the customer relationship will be a frequent driver.

Yet top management's need to keep control and its limited capacity to manage change will often stall the process of decentralisation. Shifting from top down to bottom up will meet obstacles, take different forms and proceed at a variable pace. Some radically new organisational shapes will emerge: other organisations will remain quite conventional.

Frequently, the process will be back and forth: decentralisation one moment, a more centralised approach three years later, a new round of decentralisation two years after that. Each re-organisation will be designed to correct a perceived 'over-shoot' in the previous one. 'We've been here before' will remain a familiar feeling.

Yet through all the cycles of change, the overall direction in many cases will be toward decentralisation. When 're-centralisation' occurs, commonly it will involve new forms of accountability to ensure that local units exercise their greater discretion responsibly – to further the organisation's goals. Previous models of centralisation will give way to ones that combine more local autonomy with new techniques of top management control.

Gradually, some employers will develop complex self-organising systems, with ground rules devised from above. Teams and units will have increased freedom within frameworks of values. They will rely on sophisticated systems of feedback and accountability to drive change and innovation from below.

As teams influence each other, new unexpected behaviours will have the potential to improve the organisation's performance. Creating positive and negative feedbacks to bring this about will become a senior management priority. Top managers will shift attention from managing the system to designing it, and stakeholders will expect directors (or their equivalent) to answer for the quality of system designs.

In education, for example, a pressing problem is how teachers can be encouraged to develop and keep up with best practice. Rather than constant prod and prompt from Whitehall, might the school system be redesigned? Might the Department for Education decide to treat learners as consumers – at present learners are treated more like workers ('Do the work teacher has set.')?

The Department might develop feedback mechanisms to encourage education suppliers (with teacher input) to develop learning aids for marketing direct to pupils, allowing innovation to be driven from below. Learning tools that worked would find a ready market, while those that didn't would fall by the way. Best practice would spread on the back of pupil demand.

Some organisations may increasingly devolve financial controls. Using the latest technology, small units and teams may negotiate their financial targets with other units, and have responsibility for meeting them. An organisation might effectively franchise its operations.

Might there be some organisations in which the owners of capital no longer hire managers to recruit, supervise and organise workers, but where instead it is the workers who effectively hire managers to co-ordinate, develop, finance and market their skills?

Vertical organisations will still exist, and will offer careers progressing up the ladder. Not every employer will flatten their hierarchy. As organisations decentralise, some increase in managers may be necessary to develop, implement and maintain the new systems. The price of delegation may be an increase in support, such as coaching services for staff.

Faced with competition from low-cost producers abroad, many organisations will move into higher-value activities, requiring more sophisticated – often IT based – processes. More managers seem to be associated with workplaces that are rapidly extending IT (see Chart 12.3): more complex tasks seem to demand more managers.

Chart 12.3 Change in ICT in past three years

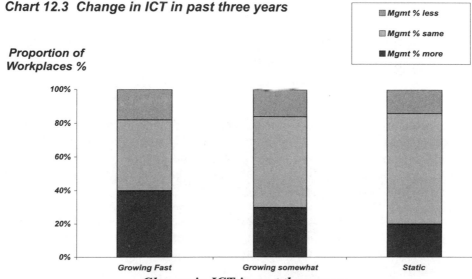

Change in ICT in past three years

Source: Michael White, Stephen Hill, Colin Mills and Deborah Smeaton, *Managing to Change?* Basingstoke: Palgrave, 2004, p. 64.

Many companies will expand to secure economies of scale, including small specialist firms that become well entrenched in a niche. Larger organisations tend to have more management grades. Will the outsourcing of HRM functions, for instance, lead to giant remuneration and HRM strategy companies, with more management layers to match their size? At a workplace level, employment growth seems to be associated with an increase in management grades (see Chart 12.4).

Chart 12.4 Growing workplaces are putting in more management grades

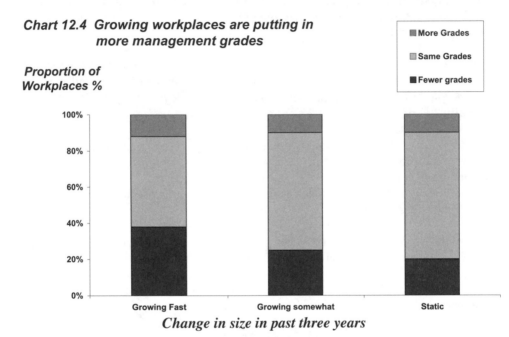

Change in size in past three years

Source: Michael White, Stephen Hill, Colin Mills and Deborah Smeaton, *Managing to Change?* Basingstoke: Palgrave, 2004, p. 62.

It is too early to predict the death of hierarchical organisations. What may well change is the function of these hierarchies. Slowly hierarchies will shift from command and control to become the designers, managers and repairers of systems that are driven from below. Straws in the wind include the upsurge of interest in coaching and the spread of consultation processes.

This changing role of hierarchies will be a key theme for the future of work. Will employees feel less stressed because they have enhanced autonomy, or more stressed because they will have too much responsibility?

The size of organisations will continue to polarize between large and small, but very gradually. In a frequently noted trend, many large organisations will become bigger as they consolidate in response to competition, and take advantage of lower transaction costs to manage operations around the world. As now, many of these organisations will combine global scale with a high degree of local autonomy – a form of 'glocalisation'.

At the same time, the number of small companies will continue to inch up.[23] Often it is start-ups that innovate and pioneer new products, as in biotechnology for instance. Some of these small companies will be micro-multinationals – relying on a handful of subcontractors in India, perhaps, and a few sales reps in Britain. Bit by bit, Britain's workforce will bifurcate between massive and very small employers.

But might this polarising trend eventually stall? As conglomerates decentralise authority to units and teams, might it become possible to combine much of the autonomy of a small company with access to all the support services of a large one? Could working for a conglomerate come to feel like working for a tiny firm, but in a networked setting?

Points to take away

• Outsourcing is unlikely to grow to the extent many predict. Employers will be more discerning in what they outsource and what they retain in-house.

• Rapid change will persist as organisations struggle to find new ways of combining control with greater decentralisation.

• As new forms of self-organisation develop, leaders will need to become experts in designing and managing systems.

---

[23] The number of companies with 1 to 49 employees increased from 956,335 in 1994 to 1,123,260 in 2003. As a proportion of all companies with employees, the figure crept up from 96.3% to 97.2%. Small Business Service.

How will work be managed?

13. Will workers be empowered or controlled?

• Work has been increasingly delegated, managers exercise less day-to-day supervision over jobs but more control over job outcomes, and work effort intensified during the 1990s.

• Employee discretion will grow as companies move up the value chain and a 'bottom up' culture spreads in society. Working in the opposite direction will be managers' limited capacity to re-design jobs radically and the lack of incentive to change among some employers.

• Organisational strategies will vary, new styles of leadership will spread, and the tension between autonomy and control will persist. Greater autonomy combined with new forms of control could increase stress.

The quest for high performance, supported by new technologies, has provoked fears that 'Taylorist' methods of factory production would spread to the office. Workers would concentrate on a narrower range of tasks, targets would be quantified more precisely, performance would be measured more exactly and employees would be subject to closer electronic monitoring. Other commentators have been more hopeful: in decentralised organisations, employer-managed jobs will give way to self-managed work, often in teams, with the employer providing support.

The debate is linked to the theme of the previous chapter. If organisations decentralise, surely they will be more inclined to empower their staff? But the connection is not simple. Management might give staff more autonomy, but use appraisals and other forms of control that workers find oppressive. Employees would have more responsibility, but not more power. So what is likely to happen over the next 20 years?

The story so far

Work has been increasingly delegated. This is clear from the 2002 survey of managers in 2000 establishments, and its companion survey of employees in the year 2000.

• 'Quality circles', in which employee groups seek to improve performance, covered three in ten workers in 2000, half as many again as in the early 1990s.

• The majority of employees worked in a group, up by 10% since 1992. Many groups had responsibility for organising their work.[1]

---

[1] Michael White, Stephen Hill, Colin Mills & Deborah Smeaton, *Managing to Change?* Basingstoke: Palgrave, 2004, pp. 45, 46.

- Cutting management layers in the 1980s and '90s, though now being somewhat reversed,[2] had increased delegation.

Yet although allowing individuals or teams to manage their own work has become a management tool, a long journey remains. A late 1990s survey of 564 UK manufacturing companies with more than 150 employees found limited evidence of much empowerment in practice. Less than a quarter claimed to empower their employees.[3]

Where quality circles and the like exist, delegation is often limited. A mid 1990s survey found that of employees who worked in groups, no more than 15% were in ones that had a 'lot of responsibility'. Compared to other European countries in the late 1990s, Britain was very much an 'average performer' in the empowerment stakes.[4]

Managers exercise less day-to-day supervision of jobs but more control over job outcomes, as work has been delegated to teams and groups. 1990s research suggests that where workers have assumed new responsibilities and have had more involvement in work organisation, managers have sought new forms of control.

Rather than detailed supervision of how the job is done, managers have exercised greater strategic control over outcomes through rigorous performance targets, peer monitoring, frequent appraisals and other forms of surveillance, often designed to maximise work effort.[5]

In 2002 nearly half the surveyed workplaces had continuous monitoring through IT. In one in five this monitoring covered all employees. However, there were signs that the technology was not being used to its full potential. Performance appraisals were also widespread, extending from white-collar staff to nearly four in ten manual workers.[6] Managers have acquired new tools to improve employee performance.

---

[2] Michael White, Stephen Hill, Colin Mills & Deborah Smeaton, *op. cit.,* p. 60-1.
[3] Robert Taylor, *Skills and Innovation in Modern Workplaces,* ESRC Future of Work Programme Seminar Series, Swindon: ESRC, 2003, pp. 16-17.
[4] John F. Geary, 'New Forms of Work Organisation. Still Limited, Still Controlled but Still Welcome?' in Paul Edwards (ed.), *Industrial Relations. Theory and Practice,* Oxford: Blackwell, 2003, pp. 344, 347.
[5] Ibid, pp. 349-52.
[6] Michael White, Stephen Hill, Colin Mills & Deborah Smeaton, *op. cit.,* pp. 86-92.

This helps to explain why many employees think they have less discretion over their jobs, despite being given more responsibility. Table 13A presents an index of task discretion, based on workers' perceptions of how much influence they have over their jobs. The index fell significantly during the 1990s, plummeting most for 'professionals' and least for 'skilled trades'.[7] Managers have delegated on the one hand, but reasserted their control – sometimes at a distance – on the other.

Table 13A Employees' Task Discretion Index has tumbled.

Year	Task Discretion Index
1992	2.43
1997	2.25
2001	2.18

Note: The Task Discretion Index is based on four questions about the amount of influence that employees thought they had over the way they did their jobs, how hard they worked, what tasks were done and how they performed those tasks. Respondents replied to each question with one of four options, ranging from 'Great Deal' to 'None'. The index is the summed average score of these answers, with a highest score of 3 and a lowest one of 0.

Source: Alan Felstead, Duncan Gallie & Francis Green, *Work Skills in Britain 1986 – 2001*, London: DfES, 2002, Table 6:1.

Work effort intensified during the 1990s, largely in response to these developments. The European Survey on Working Conditions, for example, found that across the EU[8] the proportion of workers saying they worked at very high speed or to tight deadlines climbed significantly between 1991 and 1996. Top of the table was Great Britain. High effort levels were associated with new technology, competition and low levels of worker protection (particularly through trade unions).[9]

Sometimes work intensification has been directly related to increased delegation. In the early 1990s Pirelli introduced a Total Quality programme involving job flexibility, multi-skilling and self-supervision. Effort levels went up. But in this case, greater job satisfaction accompanied work intensification. Both the employer and employees benefited.[10]

---

[7] Alan Felstead, Duncan Gallie & Francis Green, *Work Skills in Britain 1986 – 2001,* London: DfES, 2002, Table 6:4.

[8] Defined as the 12 countries who were in the EU in 1991.

[9] Francis Green and Steven McIntosh, *Working on the Chain Gang? An Examination of Rising Effort Levels in Europe in the 1990s,* Discussion Paper 465, London: LSE Centre for Economic Performance, 2000.

[10] John F. Geary, 'New Forms of Work Organisation'. *op. cit.,* p. 349.

As chapter 7 noted, the Health and Safety Executive's occupational health surveillance data suggests that work-related stress increased between 1995 and 2001/02, but has levelled off since (and may have declined).[11] Might this suggest that work effort has intensified more slowly in recent years? Or is work intensification being managed in less stressful ways?

The next 20 years

Moving up the value chain will force some employers to re-organise work. Competition from low-cost producers abroad, the need to curb costs in the public sector and the spread of best practice will encourage many, as now, to innovate.

There are obvious limits to how far organisations can compete through cost cutting alone. As they hit those limits, a growing number will be forced to compete on the basis of more specialised, high-value production, where teamwork and other high performance methods are appropriate.

In particular, many sophisticated forms of customisation will require staff to have greater autonomy. As we discussed in the last chapter, value will increasingly lie not just in what people buy, but in their process of deciding what to buy. Staff will need discretion so that they can tailor the buying experience – and often the product – to the individual.

Again as we have seen, more organisations faced by turbulent change will decentralise radically to become fleet of foot. Self-management will have an important part to play. Instead of torrents of change tumbling from above and meeting resistance, innovation will bubble upwards as empowered workers adapt to changes around them. Continuous change, driven as much by the bottom as by the top, may be easier to achieve because employees are doing much of it themselves.

These developments will swell the ranks of employers committed to high performance management. Change in this direction seems to be gathering pace. In about half the workplaces in the 2002 survey, employees had been asked to undertake a greater variety of tasks during the previous three years. The same proportion had given more training to cover for other jobs. Three in ten had increased their use of job rotation.[12] All these are aspects of high performance management.

As employees work more flexibly and with greater intelligence, detailed supervision will be unrealistic. Intelligent workers will know more about their jobs than their managers. Teams and individuals will be given more discretion.

---

[11] http://www.hse.gov.uk/statistics/causdis/stress.htm (accessed 29/3/05).

[12] Michael White, Stephen Hill, Colin Mills & Deborah Smeaton, *op. cit.*, p. 41.

In 1998 just over half of workplaces with team-working allowed members to decide jointly how the work was to be done. A mere 5% had teams that appointed their own leader.[13] These figures have almost certainly gone up, and will continue to do so. Employees will have more autonomy and will be consulted on a wider range of issues. Each step toward smart working will strengthen the case for delegation.

A *'bottom-up' culture is spreading* and will force managers to re-examine their approach. 'The end of deference' may have been prematurely celebrated as far as many workplaces are concerned, but it reflects a cultural shift that will increasingly affect work. Compared to their seniors, younger employees have better education, are more steeped in the culture of choice and expect to have greater control over their lives.

People are changing faster than many organisations. To recruit and retain the best at each skill level, as a growing number are doing, employers will have to take the expectations of young people seriously. Management culture will change gradually as 20 and 30 year olds, with their less hierarchical values, reach senior levels. A greater openness to employee empowerment will be likely.

In particular, the internet is spawning new, bottom-up ways of doing things, such as open source methodologies and blogging. These and future developments will influence how people think. Top down will feel increasingly uncomfortable. Interest in self-organising systems will continue to blossom.

As discussed in the previous chapter, 'frontier' organisations are likely to experiment with novel forms of self-organisation, requiring the effective empowerment of workers. Even now, as we have seen, in response to home-working and mobile work, some managers are relying less heavily on target setting, frequent appraisals and the like. Instead, they are creating a culture in which employees want to achieve their managers' objectives.

One organisation appraises individuals on whether they have improved a process they inherited, introduced effectively a change that impacts other staff or have developed their potential, and rewards them accordingly. Ofsted, to take a very different example, now inspects schools on a less 'coercive' basis. More emphasis is placed on working with schools to develop systems that will enable teachers to generate their own improvements. Slowly, the rhetoric of 'the learning organisation' is being turned into a reality.

These straws in the wind herald a future in which progressively innovators at the bottom will be empowered to learn and lead, taking others with them. Financial and other forms of recognition will be designed to incentivise local entrepreneurs. In some organisations, change will no longer be driven by project teams: it will be what employees do all the time.

---

[13] Mark Cully, Stephen Woodland, Andrew O'Reilly and Gill Dix, *Britain at Work,* London: Routledge, 1999, pp. 42-3.

Just as ASDA store managers have authority to innovate today, in time that authority may extend downward to check-out staff (or their 'shopping adviser' successors). Feedback systems would ensure that successful innovations were communicated to others in the store and then the company, with incentives for others to follow suit. The effects of unsuccessful experiments would be limited to the department where the idea was tried.

But limited management capacity will prove a barrier to empowerment. Turning senior and middle managers into coaches, motivators and enablers will be a huge task. So too will be designing feedback, self-monitoring and incentive systems that will enable individuals to self-manage their work and lead change from the bottom. Many of the management skills required will not exist, and will take time to learn.

Middle managers may resist the empowerment of workers below them lest they lose influence. Technology will create new opportunities to control subordinates – from devices to monitor where mobile workers travel to checks on how employees use their computers. Managers may find control a lot easier than empowerment. Retooling senior and middle management will slow the pace of change.

Offsetting this to some extent will be the growing influence of Human Resource Management (HRM) departments. Regulation – from the EU as well as Westminster – will force HRM higher up employers' agenda. Regulations on health and safety, work/life balance, diversity and employee consultation, for instance, have increased the complexity of people management, and will continue to do so.[14]

In the 2002 survey, nearly two in three workplaces (62%) reported that managers were spending more time on personnel matters than they were three years before. This was the most widespread change across the whole survey, and seems to have been due largely to increases in regulation.[15]

Stronger HR departments will have more influence on organisational strategy, more resources with which to support the introduction of HR best practice and greater awareness of developments elsewhere. They will provide something of a counter-weight to line managers who are reluctant to embrace new approaches, and a resource in helping these managers to change.

As the HR community expands and gains in status, so will its research capacity. More resources (though probably not enough) will be available to commission research on what actually works. Evidence exists that 'bundles' of changes can

---

[14] To take just three examples, legislation on age discrimination is due to take effect in October 2006, the Government is considering a further extension of parental rights, and the Health and Safety Executive will almost certainly further develop standards for measuring organisations' efforts to tackle work-related stress.

[15] Michael White, Stephen Hill, Colin Mills & Deborah Smeaton, *op. cit.,* p. 19.

bring substantial improvements in performance.[16]

Further research would expand the evidence base for best HR practice, and perhaps help HR professionals to win the support of senior colleagues. This in turn should hasten the spread of high performance management and encourage the more radical empowerment of employees.

Some employers will have little incentive to change. A large measure of empowerment will be inappropriate for many workers who lack the skills to handle greater discretion or prefer the security of tight boundaries. Firms that can make enough profit from low-paid, low-skilled and low-value processes will wonder why they should incur the costs of adopting 'high performance' methods, in which more skilled workers have greater discretion.

Britain's 'flexible labour market' may provide a relatively comfortable environment for some low-wage/low-cost employers. Especially in parts of the North where labour may be quite easily available, organisations will be able to use contract labour as and when skills are required. They will not need to invest heavily in training. They will also be able to recruit students and other temporary workers on a 'hire and fire' basis.[17]

What might be the implications?

Strategies will vary in response to these drivers – moving up the value chain, the spread of 'bottom-up' values, limited management capacity and the lack of incentive to change in some cases.

Some employers will continue with their existing approaches – but how many will survive on that basis? Others, pragmatically and cautiously, will give their employees more responsibilities. Might these employers be the majority? A growing minority will embrace more radical forms of empowerment. As more employers do this, notions of what is acceptable practice will alter and the pace of change will accelerate.

New styles of leadership will gain ground. In many organisations, styles have already evolved from 'we'll tell you' to 'we'll involve you in the decisions'. But where organisations decentralise radically, employee involvement will no longer be enough.

---

[16] John F. Geary, 'New Forms of Work Organisation', *op. cit.,* p. 353.

[17] Robert Taylor, *op. cit.,* p. 17.

Empowered workers will be workers who exercise leadership in their fields. Senior managers will find themselves leading other leaders, who will have a wide range of perspectives. Involving these employees to get 'buy in' to senior management's vision will be problematic: employees will have their own visions, and will be demotivated if views are imposed from above.

Senior managers will have to help employees negotiate their different views to achieve a common vision. Involvement in decision-making will give way to shared decision-making, a big difference. Senior managers will need skills of listening, empathy, facilitation and negotiation. They will need to develop other people rather than control them. These skills will be so demanding that they will be more likely to exist in teams of top managers than in a single 'charismatic' figure.

Genuinely shared leadership will emerge with difficulty and over time. Hierarchical approaches are deeply engrained in most organisations, and new recruits easily slip into the culture. Whole cultures have to change for very different types of leadership to take root. Some organisations will make the journey slowly, some will get stuck and others will not even start.

Authoritarian leadership, employee involvement and shared leadership will exist in different organisations over the next two decades. Shared leadership will be in the minority for most of the period, but as is starting to happen,[18] will increasingly be seen as a key to the future. But will this form of leadership make too many demands on top managers, and be superseded by another approach?

The tension between autonomy and control will persist. Managers will seek new ways of keeping control even while they expand workers' discretion. They will not trust their subordinates to exercise discretion in the best interests of the organisation, and some workers will need a guiding hand to make the best decisions.

So even more than now, for example, managers will appraise employee decision-making, using feedback from customers, peers, and senior and junior colleagues. Currently in some firms this feedback – with varying degrees of formality – is daily, weekly and monthly. The feedback is used to identify training needs, so that appraisals lead to continuous learning. Target-setting is part of the package. What is best practice now will be commonplace in future.

Many workers will welcome a well-ordered and sensitive balance between employee discretion and management control. Others will find target-setting, constant appraisal and externally imposed training irksome, and even coercive. In response, as a few are trying, some employers will seek to move from 'external' forms of control to 'internal' ones – from outside discipline to self-discipline.

---

[18] Shared leadership, in various guises, is common currency in the business schools. See for example some of the contributions in Cary L. Cooper (ed.), *Leadership and Management in the 21st Century,* Oxford: OUP, 2005.

To achieve this, a growing number will introduce new forms of appraisal, focusing less on outcomes and more on the individual's capacity to learn and improve. New methodologies to measure self-improvement will be developed. Other organisations will promote values that inspire their workforce and enable individuals to align their personal goals with those of the employer.

The hope will be that workers will not need to be told to improve their performance: they will want to do so. Management's task will be to create the culture and give employees the tools. But how many organisations will find these approaches realistic?

Greater autonomy combined with new forms of control could be a recipe for stress. On the one hand, individuals will have more responsibility, which for some will increase anxiety – 'Am I doing the job properly? Am I meeting their expectations?' This will be especially the case where expectations are ill-defined and management support is lacking. Team pressure to perform well may be a further source of stress.

On the other hand, management control may leave workers feeling disempowered – 'it's always their targets, never mine.' The decline in the 'Task Discretion Index', mentioned on page 129, indicates that more employees felt powerless during the 1990s, despite greater delegation in many organisations. If this decline continues, stress levels could mount. Lack of control is strongly associated with stress.[19]

Paradoxically, might stress and fulfilment increase together? Some of the factors that make work more satisfying are often themselves a source of stress. More challenge in a job can make you feel that you have achieved more, but it can also leave you anxious that you will fail. More autonomy can be satisfying because it stretches you, but it can leave you worried that you will let others down.

Managing work-related stress will be high on employers' agendas. Already there are signs that stress is being taken more seriously. The Health and Safety Executive, for instance, has published standards for organisations to benchmark their efforts in tackling employment-related stress.

In the 2002 survey, 38% of managers said they had or were reviewing working practices to avoid problems of stress. In the public sector the figure was just over half, while in the largest establishments it was 74%.[20] These claims may be exaggerated, but they do suggest that stress is starting to appear on managers' radar screens. As well-being gets increasing political attention, stress will move nearer to the centre of those screens.

---

[19] See for example Michael Marmot, *Status Syndrome,* London: Bloomsbury, 2004, pp. 125-28.

[20] Robert Taylor, *op. cit.,* p. 15.

Employer strategies to manage stress will include the closer monitoring of workers' emotional health, the provision of fitness rooms to encourage physical exercise (which can help to relieve stress), the provision of help lines and other forms of support, the training of managers and supervisors so that they can offer more effective support and more emphasis on developing team-working skills (since support from colleagues can be a buffer against stress).

Might the shift from 'external' to 'internal' forms of management control, and a more sophisticated search for appropriate degrees of autonomy, be part of the response too?

Greater employee discretion will put a premium on learning. Training is already a vital component of high performance management, and will be even more important in future. In particular, as more tasks are delegated to teams, improving collaborative skills will be a growing priority.

The market for training will continue to expand, with resulting shortages in high-quality trainers. These shortages will drive innovation in self-directed learning to reduce reliance on outside professionals. Learning packages, for example, will enable teams to organise their own training at ever higher levels of skill.

In some organisations continuous, self-directed personal development will become the norm, paralleling the new forms of self-assessment and self-driven learning that are beginning to appear in schools. In time, young people will have had self-improvement drilled into them at school, and will enter the workplace where constant personal development will be expected of them as well. Self-improvement will become a priority throughout their lives. How will this affect people's expectations and values? Will self-fulfilment be defined as self-improvement?

Points to take away

• Managers will continue to struggle with the tension between increasing workers' autonomy and retaining control.

• Will greater autonomy and new techniques of control add to employee stress?

• Targets will be transformed as measuring the capacity to learn and improve replaces crude measurements of output.

14. How will employees be rewarded?

• The concept of 'total reward' is gaining ground, basic pay arrangements are increasingly flexible and performance pay is widespread.

• Organisations will modify their reward strategies as they move up the value chain. Performance pay will be increasingly questioned. Tight labour markets will encourage more customised approaches. Low inflation will drive forward 'total rewards'.

• Practices will remain highly varied, reward priorities will change and more flexible savings schemes will be introduced as part of the 'total reward' concept.

Pay and benefits from work are a high priority for employees. They also matter a great deal to employers. So how workers will be rewarded could scarcely be more important. Best practice today is that reward systems – ranging from pay, to fringe benefits to working conditions – dovetail into the total HR strategy, which underpins the organisation's objectives. How will reward systems evolve over the next 20 years?

The story so far

Today's reward systems are mainly determined top down, though employees are consulted about their effectiveness. In the past, most British workers were covered by collective bargaining, allowing pay to be negotiated between management and trade unions.

The decline of unions makes this much less common today. In 1998 two-fifths of establishments with 25 or more workers were covered by collective bargaining, against an estimated four-fifths in 1960.[1] Senior managers now have much greater discretion over pay and benefits.

In the Chartered Institute of Personnel and Development's (CIPD's) 2005 annual survey of reward management (covering almost 500 UK employers), reward strategy was overwhelmingly the responsibility of the personnel/HR department and the board. Line managers, who have to implement the strategy, helped to devise it in just 28% of organisations (down from 39% in 2003). Nearly half of employers (48%) involved workers as part of the design team, through a works council or remuneration committee, or via a union or staff association.[2]

---

[1] William Brown, Paul Marginson & Janet Walsh, 'The Management of Pay as the Influence of Collective Bargaining Diminishes' in Paul Edwards (ed.), *Industrial Relations. Theory and Practice*, Oxford: Blackwell, 2003, p. 199.

[2] *Reward management: Annual survey report 2005,* London: CIPD, 2005, p. 12. *Reward management 2003,* London: CIPD, 2003, pp. 7-9.

Significantly, despite all the talk about individualising the employment relationship, in 1998 less than 5% of private sector employees negotiated pay and conditions individually with management. The vast majority of workers were covered by a standard pay and conditions package.[3]

Most large employers adopt a strategic approach to their reward practices. In the 2005 CIPD survey 45% of employers had developed, or were in the process of developing, a written reward strategy, aligned to their business and human resource strategies.

The larger the employer, the more likely they were to have an explicit strategy. 17% of organisations with fewer than 50 staff had a reward strategy, against 62% of employers with 5,000 workers or more.[4] As they grow, companies become more strategic and can afford the necessary resources. The top three reward strategy goals were 'support business goals', 'reward high performers' and 'recruit and retain high performers' (see Chart 14.1)

Chart 14.1 *Important reward strategy goals, by sector (% of respondents)*

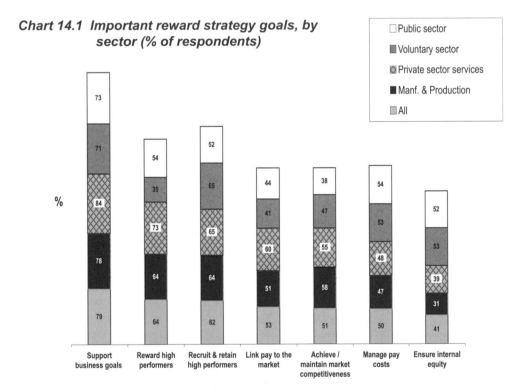

Source: *Reward management: Annual survey report 2005*, London: CIPD, 2005, p. 11.

---

[3] William Brown, Paul Marginson & Janet Walsh, *op. cit.,* p. 204.

[4] *Reward management: Annual survey report 2005,* op. cit., p. 11.

Financial rewards remain the focus of reward strategies, though the concept of 'total reward' is gaining ground. 'Total reward' seeks to extend reward beyond pay to a range of benefits, and beyond that to the work experience.[5] 28% of organisations told the CIPD survey that they had, or were in the process of adopting a 'total reward' approach. Private sector services (34%) were most likely to say this, and public services (20%) were least likely.[6]

Though menus offering employees a choice of benefits have spread, they exist in only a minority of organisations. In the 2003 CIPD survey, just 12% of employers offered them to senior managers, 11% provided them to both middle/first-line managers and white-collar non-managers, and eight per cent to manual workers.[7] They are more common in large than small organisations.[8]

Whether or not employers adopted a menu approach, the most popular benefits in the 2005 survey were paid holidays above the statutory minimum and sick pay (Chart 14.2). Among relatively new benefits were on-site massages, concierge benefits, car/bicycle loans, learning assistance and free independent advice.[9]

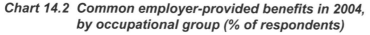

Chart 14.2 Common employer-provided benefits in 2004, by occupational group (% of respondents)

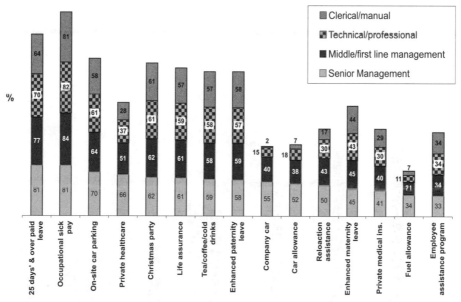

Source: *Reward management: Annual survey report 2005,* London: CIPD, 2005, p. 27.

---

[5] Paul Thompson, *Total Reward*, London: CIPD, 2002, *op. cit.,* p. 19.
[6] *Reward management: Annual survey report 2005, op. cit.,* p. 17.
[7] Ibid, pp. 15-16.
[8] Ibid, p. 27.
[9] Ibid, p. 25.

The survey report commented: 'Given that many employers are reporting difficulties in recruiting and retaining staff, it's not surprising that more employers are planning to introduce new benefits than are removing existing ones, more are increasing the value of their existing benefits than cutting it, and more are expanding the coverage of the benefit provision than reducing it.' New or expanded benefits include employee assistance programmes, designed to address stress and absenteeism.[10]

Base pay arrangements are increasingly flexible. Narrowly graded pay structures are less common than broadbanded structures for management and 'non-manual, non-management' staff, though they remain the most frequent arrangement for 'clerical/manual' workers. Broadbanded structures widen the ranges so that pay can be managed more flexibly in relation to the market (Chart 14.3).

Structures linked to individual job worth (individual rates, ranges or spots), which are usually market driven, play an increasingly important role, even covering almost a quarter of 'clerical/manual' workers.

Chart 14.3 Pay arrangements in 2004, by occupational group

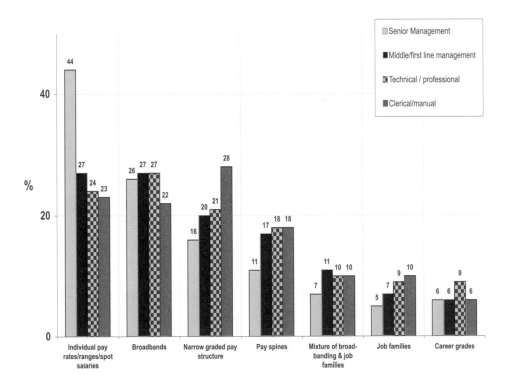

Source: *Reward management: Annual survey report 2005*, London: CIPD, 2005, p. 32.

---

[10] *Reward management: Annual survey report 2005*, op. cit., pp. 28-9.

Performance related pay is widespread. Chart 14.4 shows the criteria used to manage pay progression for various occupational groups. Despite the importance of non-performance related criteria (market rates and to a lesser extent service-related increments), performance and personal competency criteria dominate the list.

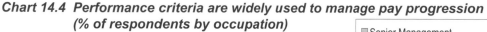

Chart 14.4 Performance criteria are widely used to manage pay progression (% of respondents by occupation)

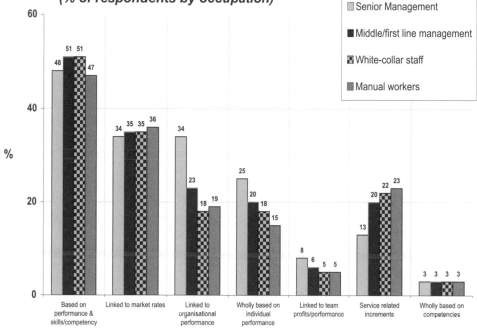

Source: *Reward management. Annual survey report 2005*, London: CIPD, 2005, p. 34.

A number of surveys have shown how performance-related pay spread in the late 1990s and early 2000s.[11] CIPD research 'shows consistently that most employers link individual progression to an assessment of an employee's performance and the skills and competencies that they apply in their job. This approach is more common in the private sector, while the public and voluntary sectors are more likely to use service-related progression.'[12]

Arrangements for relating pay to performance are increasingly varied. There is some move from individual performance to the performance of the team, department or unit. A number of employers are measuring not just outputs but inputs, such as the skills the individual brings to the job or how the job was done: was the product sold according to the ethical standards of the organisation, for example?

---

[11] Several of these are summarised by Duncan Brown, *Guide to Bonus and Incentive Plans,* London: CIPD, 2002, pp. 2-3.

[12] *Reward management: Annual survey report 2005,* op. cit., p. 32.

Just under a quarter of the CIPD sample had conducted an equal pay review between 1998 and 2003. Slightly over a quarter did the same in 2004, while two-fifths of employers planned to do so in 2005. 47% of respondents had never carried out an equal pay review.[13]

The next 20 years

Moving up the value chain will be a major influence on reward strategies over the next two decades. As organisations shift into higher quality production, their processes will change. They will require a new mix of skills, which may need to be rewarded differently too.

Some organisations will take on more knowledge workers, who will not infrequently be in short supply. A growing number of these workers will use their labour market muscle to negotiate individualised contracts that suit their personal circumstances. Many will agree flexible start and finishing times, for example, or flexibility to work at home.

Negotiating individual contracts with up to 200 people in some cases will absorb considerable management time, but smart systems will provide administrative support. Effectively, processes will be built around key workers. Other employees, in a weaker bargaining position, will slot into pre-existing structures and continue to be treated en masse. If one goes, they can be replaced by another.

An expanding group of 'high performance' employers will seek to empower their workers and develop reward systems to match. They will look for rewards that encourage employees – frequently in teams – to assume more responsibility for managing their tasks, measuring their performance and learning how to improve. Employment for some self-managed workers may increasingly feel like self-employment.

Some of these employers will develop new types of performance pay. Using smart systems, for example, budgets may be devolved, enabling employees to run their unit as a discrete profit centre, 'buying' inputs (from within the organisation or outside), 'selling' them on and retaining the profit. Instead of outsourcing a catering department for instance, might existing employees run it as an in-house co-operative?

Other 'high performance' organisations will concentrate on tying incentive pay to the most appropriate targets. As new technology swells the volume of information about performance, the challenge will be to decide which performance measures contribute most to the bottom line.

---

[13] *Reward management: Annual survey report 2005,* op. cit., pp. 41-2.

As is starting to happen, crude targets, like incentive pay linked to profits, will give way to more refined ones, such as pay linked to the measurement of customer satisfaction. Connecting performance pay to the right targets will become a priority. Management will put the organisation at risk if it gets the targets wrong.

Management perceptions about performance pay will change - slowly. Employer commitment to performance pay will remain part of the brickwork for some time because it has been in the management tradition for so long. Manufacturing managers have been wedded to payment-by-results since the 1960s, and performance pay for white collar workers has spread since the 1980s.

More recent target-setting has reinforced the tradition. As company head offices and central government have rained down targets on branches, stores or local offices, the targets have been translated into individual performance measurements, linked to performance pay. This trend will continue, with a growing emphasis – as we have seen – on linking the performance element to more appropriate targets.

But in due course this approach is likely to be challenged. Despite more information and new methodologies, pay will not always be easily aligned with the desired aspects of performance, workers may doubt the link is fair and as now, the incentive effects will frequently wear off.

Other schemes may sustain a higher level of performance, yet not be enough on their own to keep raising it.[14] You can only motivate so far with money. Indeed, too much incentive pay can destroy value, as workers may behave dysfunctionally to achieve their targets (perhaps falsifying records to suggest that targets have been met).

The challenge to performance pay is likely to be led by HRM professionals, who will be most aware of research showing the limitations of financial incentives. The need to manage employment regulation, minimise litigation and support change will mean that HRM will be increasingly well-resourced. As HRM becomes more central, its influence on overall strategy will grow. The voice against extending performance pay will be louder.

Initially HRM professionals may soften the implementation of performance pay, as can happen now. 'London' decrees that performance pay be introduced. The business unit in Manchester links the performance element to appraisals with three outcomes – 'excellent', 'satisfactory' or 'poor'. Perhaps 5%, or at most 10% of employees are to be at either extreme. The great majority are unaffected, continuing to get their normal pay rise plus increment. Performance pay turns into a vehicle for weeding out the poorest 5% - encouraging them to leave, or a first step toward dismissal.

---

[14] William Brown, Paul Marginson & Janet Walsh, *op. cit.,* p. 197.

Eventually, HRM professionals may start to challenge the notion of performance pay itself. 'Look, we know it doesn't work. There is evidence that other forms of motivation can be more effective. The company down the road trained their line managers in coaching skills, which seems to have had good results. Using appraisals to provide more targeted training has proved effective. Why don't we try something similar?'

Tight labour markets in parts of the country will influence reward strategies, too. They will force employers to pay careful attention to what their workers want. More organisations will involve employees in the design of reward systems, consult extensively before making changes and improve the feedback on what is in place.

Reward systems will continue to become more personalised, with the spread of menu approaches and more flexible hours. With customisation becoming ever more sophisticated and widespread, individuals who are used to personalisation when they are not at work will demand that managers tailor-make employment offerings in a similar way.

Skill shortages will encourage re-grading to recruit and retain labour. 'It's difficult to recruit, so let's allow people to start on grade 9 rather than 10.' Or the top 40 people in an organisation may be treated as outside the grading structure, so that the employer can roam say between £120,000 a year and £190,000 to get the individuals required.

As we have noted, shortages among low-paid workers may allow the National Minimum Wage to keep rising at a faster rate than pay in general. Trade unions and elements in government wanting to hasten Britain's shift up the value chain would support this.

But opposition will come from small and medium-sized firms, those parts of government that represent the interests of smaller firms and parts of government that fear a higher Minimum Wage would encourage employers to recruit foreign workers at below the minimum rate, adding to illegal immigration.

Today's low inflationary monetary regime has begun to impact reward systems, and will continue to do so. Every major country is now using interest rates to keep inflation at around two to three per cent, and there is little likelihood of this changing. Employers have been left with little scope for big increases in monetary wages.

More emphasis will be paid to other ingredients of the reward package, such as pensions and working conditions. Employers will ask, 'What can we do around the edge that will give us an advantage in the labour market?' This will drive forward the concept of 'total rewards'.

What might be the implications?

Practices will remain extremely varied. Yet within that diversity, three broad trends may emerge:

> • For private companies hiring knowledge workers, the market will remain paramount. Spot salaries, menu packages and other forms of personalisation will spread.

> • Within the government sector, commitment to performance pay may well persist for some time, but with the performance element a small part of the total package. In time, however, performance pay for those on middling and higher salaries will wither away, under the influence of the private sector.

> • For those at the bottom end of the labour market, changes in the National Minimum Wage will be crucial. Old-fashioned payment-by-results will persist.

Employers' reward priorities will change. In the next few years, some organisations will focus on doing incentive pay better, with more appropriate targets. Others will concentrate on personalising rewards, especially for knowledge workers. The customised workplace will become more common. But combining individualised working patterns with the growing importance of team-work, not to mention customer relations, will be a challenge.

In the long run, organisational values may be increasingly aligned to the values of the workforce. Attractive values may improve motivation and strengthen the employer's position in the labour market – 'we'll work for you because we share your values.'

Pharmaceuticals for example may see themselves not as developing and selling drugs, but as making people well. Companies with a dreary product may develop values around 'the way we work together', setting high standards for the quality of the office environment and how workers treat each other.

Might front-line staff become increasingly responsive to the values of their customers? 'Dinner ladies', following in Jamie Oliver's footsteps, might demand that children be given healthy food – 'we can't do it on 45p a person, so give us more resources.' The key role of customer relationships may give customer-facing staff considerable power. Might collective value bargaining be the long-term replacement for collective pay bargaining?

As the 'total reward' concept spreads, employers will introduce more flexible savings schemes. Workers in their twenties and thirties will have student loans to repay and mortgages to service. As now, many will find occupational pension schemes unattractive. Retirement will seem too far in the future, and immediate needs will feel more pressing.

Employers may well develop more flexible savings options in response, to gain a marginal advantage when remuneration budgets are tight. Some may contribute what they would have put into a pension to help workers pay off their mortgage. Others, in a very different section of the labour market, may encourage workers to join a credit union by making matching contributions, up to a limit.

Others again may introduce direct contribution (DC) pension schemes that allow individuals to take sums out for specified purposes before retirement. The money would have to be paid back, say within five years, to keep the employer's contribution. Innovations like these will create more customised reward packages.

Might such developments transform the savings industry? Conservative frontbench spokesman, David Willetts, has proposed a Lifetime Savings Account - LiSA. This would operate on what he calls the BOGOF principle – buy one and get one free. Every pound that the individual saved would be matched by Government, up to a certain amount. The individual would be able to withdraw their savings for a short period – but provided they paid them back, the Government's contribution would remain in the account.[15]

If employers were to develop similar arrangements, perhaps as part of DC schemes, might a new framework for savings eventually emerge? Individuals might travel through life, saving through a 'wrap-around' account that eventually became their pension pot. Employers and government would make matching contributions, up to specified amounts.

Individuals would be allowed to withdraw money to purchase 'assets' that they wanted now, but which would also boost their income in old age, such as a home or work-related learning (that would push up their income). Provided they paid the money back within a set period, they would not lose the employer and government contributions. Might this more flexible savings regime give savings a boost?[16]

Will the earnings gap between rich and poor people widen? There is strong evidence that the decline in Britain's collective bargaining widened the spread of earnings during the 1980s and '90s.[17] As unions declined, employers found it easier to tie pay rates to individual performance rather than to the job. This allowed differentials to widen, traditional comparabilities to be eroded and groups of workers to fall behind if their market position weakened.

With collective bargaining most unlikely to return (see the next chapter), this long-term trend will be difficult to reverse. Might it be softened, however, were the National Minimum Wage to rise faster than average earnings?

---

[15] Jesse Norman & Greg Clark, *Towards a Lifetime of Saving*, London: Conservative Research & Development, 2004.

[16] For details on how such a scheme might work, see Michael Moynagh & Richard Worsley, *Opportunity of a Lifetime: Reshaping Retirement,* London: CIPD, 2004, pp. 112-35.

[17] Some of the evidence is summarised by William Brown, Paul Marginson & Janet Walsh, *op. cit.,* pp. 207-9.

Points to take away

• Some organisations will align incentive pay more closely to elements that are vital for performance. Others will move away from incentive pay altogether.

• Non-pay elements of reward will loom larger in employers' thinking, such as innovative savings schemes, support for housing costs, and creating a healthy and attractive work environment.

15. Do trade unions have a future?

> • Trade union membership has declined, employees are being consulted in alternative ways and legally enforceable rights at work have been greatly extended.
>
> • A strong union resurgence is unlikely because employment growth will be concentrated in private services where unions account for just 15% of employees, unions will remain unfashionable especially among young people and unions will struggle to find new, more attractive roles.
>
> • The transition from employee protection based on collective agreements to protection based on individual statutory rights looks set to continue. Good employers will seek to be ahead of the regulatory game. Effective employee communication will be even more vital.

The days of strikes, mass picketing and dramatic TUC visits to No. 10 seem aeons away. The balance of power has shifted from labour to capital since the 1970s, due to Thatcherite trade union reforms and globalisation: many unionised jobs have been offshored, other employees fear their jobs will be next and unions have proved notoriously bad at organising internationally.

It is often said that Britain's 'voluntary' system of collective bargaining between unions and employers is now giving way to employment relations based on minimum statutory rights – workers are increasingly protected not by unions, but by law. This could be one of the most profound changes to impact the workplace. Is it a long-term trend?

The story so far

Trade union influence has waned over the past quarter century. Union membership plummeted from almost half the workforce in 1980 to just over a quarter in 2000 (see Chart 15.1), largely reflecting the contraction of manufacturing, a union stronghold.

Following the 1999 Employment Relations Act, which made it a little easier for unions to get recognition, this decline has been slightly reversed. Over 1000 agreements brought 250,000 new workers under union recognition between 2000 and 2002.[1] Total membership – both in numbers and as a proportion of the UK workforce – remained much the same during the following year, but fell by 0.5% in 2003-04.[2]

---

[1] David Metcalf, 'Trade unions' in Richard Dickens, Paul Gregg and Jonathan Wadsworth (eds), *The Labour Market Under New Labour,* Basingstoke: Palgrave, 2003, p. 186.

[2] Tom Palmer, Heidi Grainger & Grant Fitzner, *Trade Union Membership 2003,* DTI, 2004, available at http://www.dti.gov.uk/er/emar/tum2003.pdf; Heidi Grainger & Heather Holt, *Trade Union Membership 2004,* DTI, 2005, available at http://www.dti.gov.uk/er/emar/tradeunion_membership2004.pdf.

Membership has dwindled most in the private sector, though this could change as government seeks to cut the number of civil servants in administrative and support roles by a gross 84,000 by 2007-08.[3] Three in five public sector employees belonged to a union in the early 2000s, against one in five in the private sector.

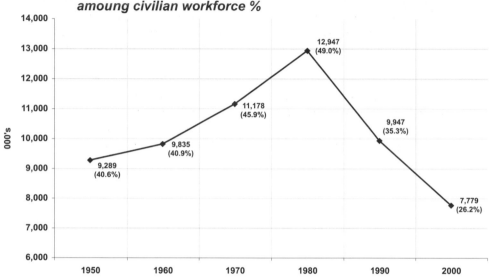

Chart 15.1 Trade union membership 000's and density amoung civilian workforce %

Source: David Metcalf, 'Trade unions' in Richard Dickens, Paul Gregg and Jonathan Wadsworth (eds), *The Labour Market Under New Labour,* Basingstoke: Palgrave, 2003, p. 171.

Trade unions have fewer opportunities to bargain on pay. A quarter of union members are not covered by collective agreements for their pay. In the 1990s one in three private sector workplaces abandoned collective bargaining (though many continued to hold formal discussions with unions on other matters).

Perhaps more significant is that most new workplaces don't have collective bargaining. In 1998 unions were recognised for pay bargaining at 32% of workplaces that had been around for 25 years or more, at 22% that had existed for 10 to 24 years and at only 18% established within the previous decade.[4]

---

[3] Sir Peter Gershon, *Releasing Resources to the Frontline. Independent Review of Public Sector Efficiency,* London: The Stationery Office, 2004.
[4] Mark Cully, Stephen Woodland, Andrew O'Reilly & Gill Dix, *Britain at Work*, London: Routledge, 1999, pp. 238-41.

Unions have continued to merge, mainly as a result of their declining influence. A hundred years ago there were 1,300 unions, after the Second World War 800 and by 2002 the figure was 226. Eleven unions, each with over 250,000 members, now account for almost three quarters of the total membership.[5] Amicus, Britain's largest union, and the Transport and General Workers Union are currently discussing a merger.

Employees are being consulted in alternative ways. As trade unions have played a smaller part in representing workers to management, 'direct' forms of consultation such as team briefings, regular meetings between senior management and the workforce, and problem-solving groups have played a larger role.

Employers have also been under a stronger obligation to consult employees 'indirectly', through representatives of the workforce. In a landmark judgement in 1994, the European Court of Justice ruled that EU information and consultation measures applied to employers whether or not they recognised trade unions.

This required UK law to provide for the election of issue-specific employee representatives in certain circumstances. Piecemeal legislation has subsequently provided for these elections, where employees want them and unions are not recognised, in areas such as health and safety, working time and parental leave.

Then came the European Works Councils Directive, incorporated into UK law in 1999. This gave UK employees in companies operating across the Union statutory rights to information and consultation on key business, employment and restructuring matters.

The latest and most far-reaching development stems from the 2002 EU Directive on Information and Consultation, which the UK will implement in stages from March 2005. For the first time, Britain will have a comprehensive, generally applicable statutory framework obliging employers to inform and consult employees or their representatives on a range of business, employment and restructuring issues.[6]

Together, these developments mean that alternative channels are beginning to supplement Britain's 'single channel' approach to employee representation, relying on trade unions. Direct forms of consultation (management to workforce) are combining with indirect mechanisms, involving management and employee representatives.

> • In 1984, two thirds (67%) of workplaces with 25 or more employees had 'union only' or 'union and non-union' arrangements for listening to employees. In 1998 the proportion had fallen to two-fifths (42%).

---

[5] David Metcalf, *op. cit.,* p. 173.

[6] Mark Hall & Mike Terry, 'The Emerging System of Statutory Worker Representation' in Geraldine Healy, Edmund Heery, Phil Taylor & William Brown, *The Future of Worker Representation,* Basingstoke: Palgrave, 2004, pp. 207-28.

• In 1984 a mere 17% of workplaces had arrangements classified as 'non-union only', but by 1998 this had more than doubled to 40%. Nearly all new workplaces opted for direct communication methods without recognising unions.

• The number of unions reporting 'no voice' – ie no formal communication arrangements with trade unions – remained constant (16% in 1984 and 17% in 1998).[7]

Legally enforceable individual rights at work have been greatly extended, again mostly arising from the EU's social market agenda. These rights include the regulation of working time; equal rights with full-time, permanent employees for part-time, temporary or sub-contracted workers; minimum rights for migrant, women and disabled workers; and in the pipeline stronger rights for older workers.

The landscape of industrial relations is being transformed. In the past regulation created a broad framework of minimum collective rights, within which different voluntary initiatives could suit a variety of workplaces. Today, a diversity of voluntary approaches is increasingly set within a statutory framework of minimum individual rights.

The next 20 years

Will this be the trend for the next 20 years? Or might unions re-invent themselves and take employee relations in a different direction? A strong union resurgence is improbable – for a number of reasons.

The growth in union membership between 2000 and 2002 appears to be unsustainable. The expansion was largely a response to legislation that came into effect in June 2000, making it easier for unions to gain legal recognition. Though between then and December 2002 fewer then 20,000 workers got recognition by appealing to the law, the threat of compulsion seems to have encouraged a significant number of employers to recognise a union.

However, this was largely in industries where unions were already strong – notably (ex-) public services, manufacturing, finance, and transport and communication.

---

[7] David Metcalf, *op. cit.,* p. 174. 'Union only' was defined as one or more trade unions recognised by employers for pay bargaining, or a joint consultative committee meeting at least once a month with representatives chosen through trade union channels. 'Union and non-union' were a combination of 'union only' with other arrangements, such as problem-solving groups of meetings with non-union employee representatives. 'No voice' was defined as a joint consultative committee meeting at least once a month with representatives not chosen through union channels, regular meetings between senior management and the workforce, briefing groups, problem-solving groups, or non-union employee representatives. 'Union and non-union' arrangements were a combination of these.

Only one in six newly covered workers were in the rest of the private sector.[8]

Yet employment growth is likely to be weak in sectors where unions have traditionally been strong. The government plans large reductions in civil servants over the next few years, manufacturing employment appears to be in long-term relative decline, a growing number of jobs in the financial services are being relocated overseas and there is no hint of an employment surge in the utilities or transport.

Employment growth is likely to be concentrated in private services, where unions account for just 15% of employees. Despite the soon-to-be-slowed surge in public sector jobs since 1998, the overwhelming majority of the three million jobs created from 1991 to March 2004 were in the private sector.[9]

Some unions have developed innovative approaches to recruit these workers, many of whom are in small enterprises, self-employed, part-time or temporary. But despite some success, these efforts have not been enough to reverse the unions' overall decline.

A fundamental problem is the fragmented nature of many services. Even if they obtained bargaining rights, unions would find it extremely difficult to negotiate standard terms and conditions with numerous 'disorganised' employers in a sector. Union rates can be undercut by non-unionised employers, weakening unions' bargaining power and reducing the incentive to join.[10]

Recruiting and servicing a fragmented workforce puts considerable pressure on a limited number of officials. There are now only an estimated 5000 full-time union officers.[11] These officials have traditionally concentrated on larger workplaces. Making contact with workers in smaller units will represent a 'tax' on existing members, who will either have to pay more or see their officials less often.

The ratio of officers to members in unions with workers spread across small worksites is comparatively high. Organising new groups of workers often diverts resources from elsewhere. The T & G's campaign to recruit workers at Manpower was led by two full-time officers, seconded from other duties.[12] Growing a union can weaken the home base. The creative use of electronic communications will only partly solve these difficulties.

---

[8] William Brown & Sarah Oxenbridge, 'Trade Unions and Collective Bargaining: Law and The Future of Collectivism' in Catherine Barnard, Simon Deakin and Gill Morris, (eds.) *The Renewal of Labour Law,* 2003 pp. 63-78.

[9] David Smith, 'Relax, there is no need to be gloomy about jobs', *The Sunday Times,* 22 May 2005.

[10] This has been an obstacle to the organisation of agency workers, for example. See Edmund Heery, 'The trade union response to agency labour in Britain', *Industrial Relations Journal,* 35(5), 2004, p. 448.

[11] Robert Taylor, *The Future of Employment Relations,* ESRC Future of Work Seminar Series, Swindon: ESRC, 2003, p. 18.

[12] Edmund Heery, Hazel Conley, Rick Delbridge & Paul Stewart, 'Beyond Enterprise? Trade Unions and the Representation of Contingent Workers', *Future of Work Series – Working Paper 7,* Leeds: ESRC Future of Work Programme, n.d., pp. 19-20.

In their existing guise, unions will remain unattractive, especially to young people.

> • In 2000 a mere 18% of workers aged 18 to 29 belonged to a union, compared to 44% in the early 1980s. The figure for the private sector, where 83% of that age group worked, was just 11%. Many young people regard unions as backward-looking, middle-aged and male-dominated – 'pale, male and stale'.[13]

> • Of the 36% of workers covered by a collective agreement on pay, over one third (14%) are free-riders: they don't belong to a union. They get the benefits of union membership without having to pay the subscription to join. The incentive for them to become members is small.[14]

> • The benefits from joining a union may be less than in the past. In the 1970s and '80s workers received higher pay if they were unionised, but recent research suggests that this pay premium has disappeared for men, and has fallen significantly for women.[15]

Many people join unions because their friends and colleagues belong. Black members' networks, for example, have drawn black women into unions in workplaces that were already well-organised.[16] But these networks can also be excluding. They seem to have put off Asian women, who do not see themselves as 'black'.[17]

More generally, if 'my sort of people' don't belong to a union, recruitment will be difficult. Networks will support unions where unions are strong, but in workplaces with no union presence networks of non-union workers will reinforce the impression that 'unions are not for us'. Getting a foothold in these networks will remain a huge challenge for union officials.

---

[13] Robert Taylor, *op. cit.,* p. 13.

[14] David Metcalf, *op. cit.,* p. 183.

[15] Ibid, p. 178-9.

[16] Geraldine Healy, Harriet Bradley & Nupur Mukherjee, 'Getting In – Getting Active: The Experience of Minority Ethnic Women in Trade Unions', *Future of Work Series – Working Paper 29,* Leeds: ESRC Future of Work Programme, 2003.

[17] Harriet Bradley, Geraldine Healy & Nupur Mukherjee, 'Inclusion, Exclusion and Separate Organisation – Black Women Activists in Trade Unions', *Future of Work Series – Working Paper 25,* Leeds: ESRC Future of Work Programme, 2002, pp. 17-8.

Unions will struggle to find new, more attractive roles. Though the pay advantages from belonging to a union are less than they were, unionised workplaces are still more likely to have some form of equal opportunities policy, family friendly policies and fewer industrial accidents.[18] Might unions gain a new lease of life by extending the range of benefits available to members?

Unions with high numbers of freelance workers, for example, offer dedicated services such as finance and taxation advice, opportunities for professional and business development, information about job vacancies, sickness benefits and pensions. Other unions offer consumer services, such as special mortgages for workers on fixed-term contracts[19]

The trouble is that employers are doing the same. Using flexible remuneration systems, a growing number offer cheap insurance and other deals. Many collaborate through 'portal purchasing' to secure economies of scale – a group of large companies will have enough workers to secure substantial discounts. They can almost match the scale economies obtained through union mergers.

Partnership agreements will not stem the decline in union membership, despite the hopes of some union officials. In a move away from adversarial industrial relations, unions are signing these agreements to become partners with employers, providing support in managing the organisation.

Employers are worried by the escalating number of appeals to industrial tribunals in defence of workers' statutory rights. With the potential extension of these rights through European legislation, the potential costs of litigation are enormous. Might unions help employers by representing individuals through procedures that avoid litigation?

There are few signs of workplaces with no tradition of union recognition embracing such an approach. Where partnership agreements do exist, the evidence is ambiguous. In nine recent case studies across a range of industries, union officials said that consultations on pay felt like negotiations – some even had ballots. But managers claimed that they were no more than consultations since the pay figure had been determined by senior management.

Both sides most appreciated the informal relationships, which enabled managers to use union officials as a sounding board and officials to represent workers off the record. In companies with weak union roots, partnerships were more like a chimera.[20]

---

[18] Michael White, Stephen Hill, Colin Mills & Deborah Smeaton, *Managing to Change?*, Basingstoke: Palgrave, 2004.

[19] Edmund Heery, Melanie Simms, Hazel Conley, Rick Delbridge & Paul Stewart, *op. cit.,* p. 9.

[20] William Brown and Sarah Oxenbridge, 'Achieving a new equilibrium? The stability of cooperative employee-union relationships', paper presented to *Future of Work. The 2nd International Colloquium,* Leeds, 9-10 September 2004.

Where partnership agreements do prove effective, they may actually weaken the unions. In one NHS trust, partnership with management at the trust level exhausted union energies and resources in servicing the central institutions. Union officials had less time to support individual members and grew increasingly remote.[21]

More probable is that instead of partnership agreements, mediation processes will be further developed to avoid recourse to the law. An army of HR consultants will be available to bring aggrieved individuals and managers together, to facilitate tense meetings of consultative committees, to coach managers in conflict resolution and to help develop processes that enhance employee satisfaction. When 'the piper calls the tune', why should employers rely on unions to help resolve differences rather than HR managers and consultants?

Workers will have new rights to be informed and consulted under the EU Directive on Information and Consultation. When the directive is fully implemented in March 2008, British workers in undertakings of at least 50 employees will be entitled to receive information and be consulted, through workplace consultative committees, on a much wider range of issues than is currently the case. Negotiating arrangements for this will need to be triggered by at least 10% of employees or by management.

This potentially will give workers an alternative to trade unions through which to express views on the running of their organisation. Also encouraging this second channel could be the 'apparent growth of employer interest in developing systems of employee consultation as a means toward improved corporate performance.'[22] Non-union firms like Pizza Express and B & Q have recently established elaborate consultation mechanisms, for example. The 'end of deference' means that managers from 'Generation X', with their individualistic and less hierarchical values, could be more inclined to adopt a consultative approach.

Yet new arrangements for informing and consulting employees will take time to develop. Many workers will not be aware of their rights. They may be apathetic, especially where direct communication between management and workers (without employee representatives) works well. Managers may prefer to improve these direct channels to avoid spending extra time in new consultative mechanisms. Individuals may hesitate to take the lead in requesting new arrangements or being actively involved in them when they are established, lest their promotion prospects suffer.

---

[21] Stephanie Tailby, Mike Richardson, Paul Stewart, Andy Danford & Martin Upchurch, 'Partnership at work and worker participation: an NHS case study', *Industrial Relations Journal*, 35(5), 2004, pp. 403-18.

[22] Mark Hall & Mike Terry, 'The Emerging System of Statutory Worker Representation', *op.cit*, p. 223.

Even so, when fully implemented, the Directive on Information and Consultation is likely to accelerate developments already afoot.

- Five per cent of workplaces with five employees or more surveyed in 2002 planned to introduce a consultative committee for the first time during the following year.

- A further nine per cent, with some consultative arrangements already, planned to extend them.

- Many of these planned developments were in smaller workplaces, and three quarters in non-unionised ones.[23]

What might be the implications?

The transition from employee protection based on collective agreements to protection based on individuals' statutory rights is set to continue. Trade union influence will remain at today's low ebb, and perhaps wane further. Statutory regulation will have an increasing role, especially as well-being rises up the political agenda. Employers will be expected to protect individuals' well-being at work.

More rights-based legislation will be welded on to Britain's voluntary tradition in industrial relations. As now, this legislation will seek to strengthen the framework of workers' rights, while giving employers maximum discretion in how the law is implemented.

Good employers will seek to be ahead of the regulatory game, as they seek to become employers of choice, often in tight labour markets. They will spot what is coming by way of regulation and prepare to implement it effectively. They will seek to create working conditions that are imaginative, are over and above regulatory obligations, sustain a good employment brand and help to avoid employee litigation.

To help them achieve this, they will invest in more sophisticated and better resourced HRM. They will pioneer or copy new concepts and methodologies. Practices will become less piecemeal and more systemic. Rather than addressing individual issues discretely – such as recruitment, training, pensions, and family friendly initiatives – more attention will be paid to the design of integrated HR systems. By 2025 might HRM finally have given teeth to the mantra, 'people are our most important asset'?

---

[23] Michael White, Stephen Hill, Colin Mills & Deborah Smeaton, *op. cit.*, pp. 162-3.

Effective forms of employee consultation will be vital as organisations move up the value chain. As the 2003 European Commission Davignon report explained:

> 'Globalisation of the economy and the special place of European industry raises fundamental questions regarding the power of the social partners within the company. The type of labour required by European companies – skilled, mobile, committed, responsible and capable of using technical innovations and of identifying with the objective of increasing competitiveness and quality – cannot be expected to obey the employer's instructions. Workers must be closely and permanently involved in decision-making at all levels of the company.'[24]

Constant waves of company mergers and acquisitions, the inherent instability of consumer, product and financial markets, and the rapid transmission of best practice mean that organisations will face the imperative of almost constant change. Changes are most effectively introduced when there is employee consent, based on transparent information and consultation procedures.

A growing number of western European countries, including Germany, Finland and Sweden, are encouraging workplace development programmes, negotiated between employers and employees and involving the state where necessary. This approach promises a new form of social contract at work that puts mutual consent at the heart of corporate modernization and change.[25]

In the UK, UNISON's 'learning parternships' illustrate the potential for employers and workforce representatives to collaborate in the raising of skills. These partnerships have encouraged a substantial number of workers with few opportunities to access employer-provided training and development.[26]

When today's individualistic younger people with less respect for authority begin to dominate the workplace, will British managers put employee involvement at the centre of their employment strategies?

---

[24] Cited by Robert Taylor, *Partnerships at Work. The Way to Corporate Renewal?*, ESRC Future of Work Programme Seminar Series, Swindon: ESRC, 2004, p. 17.

[25] Ibid, p. 14.

[26] Anne Munro & Helen Rainbird, 'Opening doors as well as banging on tables: an assessment of UNISON/employer partnerships on learning in the UK public sector', *Industrial Relations Journal,* 35(5), 2004, pp. 419-33.

Points to take away

• Trade unions are unlikely to make much of a come-back, not least because they will struggle to break into the networks of non-unionised employees.

• More legislation protecting workers' rights will be welded on to Britain's voluntary tradition of industrial relations.

• Employee involvement will be a higher management priority.

What balance will be
struck between work and 'life'?

16. Will people spend less time at work?

> • The long-term fall in weekly hours of work has resumed since the late 1990s, though the picture for holidays has been more mixed.
>
> • Rising affluence and the demand for a better work-life balance will increase the demand for more leisure. Yet international competitive pressures may work the other way.
>
> • Contracted working time is likely to fall, but will this take the form of a shorter working week or longer holidays? Formal cuts in working time may be offset by more people working long hours informally.

The age of extended leisure has long been predicted. Might we take a big step toward it over the next 20 years? As 'globalisation' makes the more developed world even more prosperous, the historic trend for greater wealth to be taken partly in more leisure could persist. If this happens, will extra leisure take the form of a shorter working week or longer holidays? On the other hand, 'globalisation' could so intensify international competition that cost pressures rule out cuts in working time. Which is more likely?

The story so far

In the mid nineteenth century British men typically worked for at least 55 hours a week. Their hours dropped significantly around the First World War, and again fell from the 1950s. The decline came to an abrupt end after 1981.[1]

The fall in weekly hours has resumed since the late 1990s – at least for men. As Chart 16.1 shows, the average weekly hours usually worked by full-time male employees has decreased gently from a post-1983 peak of 45.8 hours in the second quarter of 1997 to 44.3 hours in the same quarter of 2004. The figure for women remained broadly stable in the mid to late 1990s, but has inched down by half an hour since 2001.

---

[1] Francis Green, 'The Demands of Work' in Richard Dickens, Paul Gregg & Jonathan Wadsworth, *The Labour Market Under New Labour. The State of Working Britain 2003*, London: Palgrave, 2003, p. 140.

Chart 16.1 Usual weekly hours since 1983 (Average number of usual weekly hours in main job, all occupations, UK employees, full time, male and female, annual, quarter2)

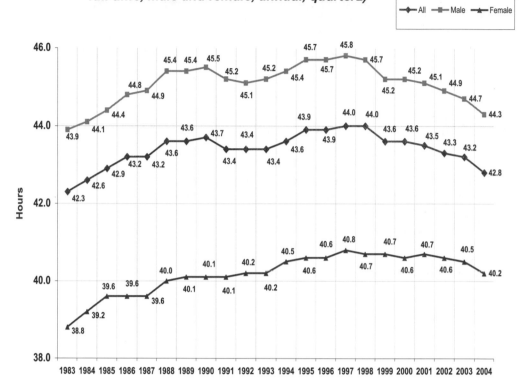

Source: *Eurostat Labour Force Survey,* Table EWHUNA, updated 6 April 2004.

The drop in male workers' hours started more or less when the European Directive on Working Time was implemented in 1998. This would suggest that the Directive has had a significant impact, despite its opt-out clause, which currently allows people to work more than a 48-hour week if they choose. Are we witnessing the start of a new long-term trend to shorter working hours?

Despite the modest shrinkage of the working week, Britain's 'long hours culture' remains top of the European league (Chart 16.2). In 2004 British full-time workers spent almost two and a half hours a week longer on the job than the European average – an improvement on 2001, however, when the gap was about three and a quarter hours.

Chart 16.2 Usual hours worked per week, full-time employees, 2004 (Average number of usual weekly hours in main job, all occupations, UK employees, full time, male and female)

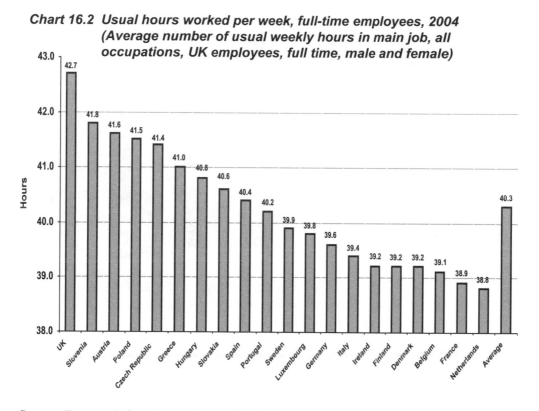

Source: *Eurostat Labour Force Survey,* Table EWHUNA, updated 6 April 2004.
Note: all figures are for quarter 3, except Luxembourg (which is quarter 4, 2003) and Germany (quarter 2, 2003).

The picture for holidays has been more mixed. In the 1980s and '90s holiday entitlements increased for many workers – but not everyone. In 1986 the legal minimum holiday rights in Wages Council industries were abolished. This left about one in ten workers – mainly women – in low-paid industries, not covered by collective bargaining, with no holiday rights.

However, the Working Time Directive has more than halved this figure (see Chart 16.3). In particular, the proportion of women deprived of any entitlement to holidays nose-dived from 15% in 1996 to 6% in 2001.[2] The Directive entitles full-time workers to four weeks paid leave a year, which may include the eight bank holidays. Part-time workers are entitled to the same on a pro rata basis.

---

[2] Francis Green, *op. cit.,* pp. 142-3. The proportion of women deprived of any entitlement to holidays fell from 15% in 1996 to 6% in 2001.

Chart 16.3 Proportion of workers with no paid holiday rights

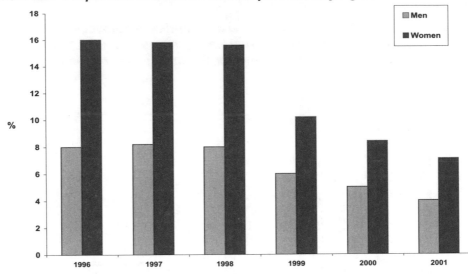

Source: Source: Francis Green, 'The Demands of Work' in Richard Dickens, Paul Gregg & Jonathan Wadsworth, *The Labour Market Under New Labour. The State of Working Britain 2003,* London: Palgrave, 2003, p. 143.

As Chart 16.4 shows, the UK is near the bottom of the European league in the number of paid holidays stipulated under collective agreements. At 26.5 days in 2003, the average for the EU and Norway had increased by one day since 2000 (though the countries included and the calculation methods are not exactly comparable).

Chart 16.4 Average collectively agreed annual paid leave (in days) 2003

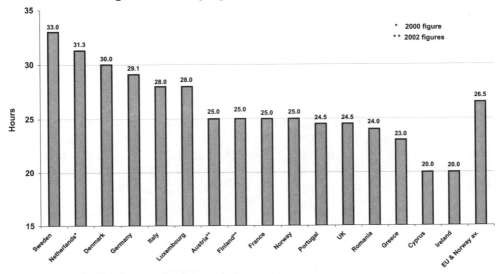

Source: http://www.eiro.eurofound.eu.int/2004/03/update/tn0403104u.html

The next 20 years

Rising affluence will be a key influence on working time. Over the past 30 years, per capita incomes grew at an average of 2.5% a year in the more developed countries. Should this continue, which many commentators think is a reasonable assumption, average incomes would be around 60% higher in 20 years and would have doubled within 28 years.[3]

Experts generally attribute past falls in working time to increased affluence: people prefer to take part of their greater wealth in more leisure. All things being equal, higher prosperity in the more developed world will make possible cuts in working time – and why should Britain buck the trend?

Work-life balance will remain firmly on the agenda, as society continues to expect more of parents.[4] As now, this will translate into parental demands to have more time and energy for children. High childcare costs, due to a shortage of carers, will reinforce these demands, despite state subsidies for childcare (discussed in the next chapter).[5]

Shorter hours or longer holidays could make it easier for both parents to work full-time, with fewer stressful effects on the home. Part-time work for one partner may not be practical where couples want to maintain their earnings or where employers – in tight labour markets – would struggle to fill the other 'half' of the job.

Might longer weekends or extra holidays help organisations to combat work-related stress? In particular, might cuts in working time help employers attract and retain 'worn and torn' older workers, a growing number of whom may need to stay in employment for financial reasons but would find full-time work, on current hours, difficult to manage?[6]

---

[3] Roger Bootle, *Money for Nothing,* London: Nicholas Brealey, 2003, p. 254. Obviously, this is a huge assumption., yet some commentators would say it is quite cautious.

[4] For example, parents are spending more on their children in terms of time and money, and they are more anxious to be good parents. Michael Willmott & William Nelson, *Complicated Lives,* London: Wiley, 2003, pp. 145-160.

[5] One study estimated that universal childcare for one to four year olds in the UK would require around 1.5 million additional full-time equivalent places to be created with child care providers, at a total cost of nearly £10 billion (at 2003 prices). Based on the Scandinavian model, if government met three quarters of these extra costs and parents the rest, the initial net cost to the Exchequer – after allowing for the extra tax revenue from the additional jobs created – would be just under £3 billion p.a. 'Universal childcare provision in the UK – towards a cost-benefit analysis', PricewaterhouseCoopers, August 2003.

[6] Some older workers see intense forms of work as a major barrier to continued employment. See for example Donald Hirsch, *Crossroads after 50. Improving choices and work in retirement,* York: Jospeh Rowntree Foundation, 2003, p. 26.

International competition will limit cuts in working time: companies will be reluctant to put themselves at a disadvantage against Asian and other competitors with lower labour costs. Overseas competition has forced French and German employers to start rowing back on earlier reductions in working time. Might this point to long-term constraints on all the more advanced economies?

On the other hand, employers who are sheltered from global competition may find it easier to trim working time. Might these sectors take the lead, forcing others to follow? Companies that resist cuts because of international competition may include some that will offshore anyway. As the UK moves out of activities that can be transferred to the industrialising world, might companies opposed to contractions in working time diminish? Or will the race up the value chain mean that Asian competitors will always be nipping at Britain's heels, curbing increases in leisure?

Skill shortages could put workers in the driving seat, forcing employers to concede longer holidays or shorter hours. But equally, cuts in working time could tighten labour markets further: Unless they got compensating productivity improvements, employers would have to recruit extra workers to cover for the shorter hours or longer holidays.

What might be the implications?

On balance, it is likely that contracted working time will continue to drop, if slowly and intermittently.

But what balance will be struck between shorter hours and longer holidays? Will employers see a cut in hours as the opportunity to introduce new shift patterns – four longer working days a week, for example, with three day weekends? Will they shorten the working week in return for more flexible hours – to help them respond to the 24/7 consumer perhaps?

Or will they prefer to bunch working time reductions into longer holidays, maybe at 'low' periods of the year (for example, a week after Christmas)? Will annual hours budgets spread, possibly linked to menu-based reward packages – 'you can trade off more pay for less working time', or 'you can bid for the hours you want to work, and in return for working the least popular hours you can have more time off'?

Will 'formal' reductions in working time be offset by more people working long hours informally - taking work home in the evenings or at weekends? This could come about through an increase in the amount of discretion individuals have over their work, more mobile work that blurs the distinction between work and home and advances in technology that make it easier for people to work remotely, 'out of hours'.

In Silicon Valley, for example, mobile phones and other technologies enable individuals to be permanently connected to their jobs, often merging work with the rest of life. Formal working hours have less relevance.[7] Around the world, a growing minority take laptops and mobile phones with them on holiday.

The demand for recreation products will grow strongly as leisure expands and incomes increase. Extra holidays would give a fillip to the holiday industry, obviously. In particular, longer weekends would boost the market for weekend trips – both within Britain and abroad. What would happen to transport congestion at beauty spots and airports?

The 24/7 society would spread further if shorter hours took the form of more flexible shifts. More workers on evening and weekend shifts would increase the number of people shopping in out of 'normal' hours, which in turn would create even more demand for flexible shifts. Might shifts become so variable that 'the weekend' becomes a thing of the past?

Points to take away

> • Statutory working time will shrink gradually, but more people may work long hours informally.
>
> • Will cuts in working time take the form of a shorter working week or longer holidays?

---

[7] Howard Rhiengold, *Smart Mobs. The Next Social Revolution,* Cambridge MA: Basic Books, 2002, p. 191.

17. Flexibility for whom?

> • Employer and employee forms of flexibility are widespread, when viewed together. But traditional flexibility for employers may be hitting a ceiling, while flexibility for employees remains limited.
>
> • Constraints on employers will be a bigger influence on the future than employees' desire for more flexibility. Public policy will be critical. Many organisations will give a higher priority to 'intelligently flexible' methods of work.
>
> • Flexibility for employers and employees may be slowly modified. Work-life balance will continue to be problematic, with damaging effects on individuals' well-being.

Flexible labour markets arc widely seen as a strength of the British economy – but flexibility for whom? Employees ideally want the flexibility to choose the number of hours they work, when they work them and whether to take extended leave. But when some employers talk about flexibility they mean the freedom to hire and fire workers, employ them on a variety of contractual terms and require them to work unsocial hours.

These differences lie at the heart of the struggle over work-life balance. At present, 'Britain's flexible labour market' refers to flexibility for employers more than employees, and many people don't like it. They wish there was something better. Will the employer view continue to prevail, or will the employee perspective gain ground?

The story so far

Employer and employee forms of flexibility are widespread, when added together. 'If we define a "standard" job as one where individuals work at the employer's premises during the day and for 30-48 hours a week, only 41% of men and 40% of women hold "standard" jobs.' Based on the British Household Panel Survey, in the 1990s employees in non-standard, flexible employment included:[1]

- About 8% of all workers not on permanent contracts.

- Almost 15% who spent some time working from home, travelling or working in more than one place.

- About 30% who had non-standard times, such as afternoons and evenings, and weekends.

---

[1] Alison L. Booth & Jeff Frank, 'Gender and Work-Life Flexibility in the Labour Market' in Diane M. Houston (ed.), *Work-Life Balance in the 21ˢᵗ Century,* Basingstoke: Palgrave, 2005, pp. 16-7.

- About 40% who had non-standard hours, such as less than 30 hours or more than 48 hours a week.

- An unspecified proportion who combined two or more of these.

Traditional flexibility for employers appears to be hitting a ceiling. In the 2002 survey of 2000 establishments, four in five workplaces used at least one of the following: temporary staff supplied by agencies, their own temporary employees, workers employed on a casual basis, freelance (self-employed) workers, and homeworkers or outworkers.[2]

But Chart 17.1 shows that the number of workplaces with recent increases in these types of flexible labour was almost offset by the number cutting back. The main exception – home or outworkers – included existing employees starting to work at, or from home for at least part of their time.

Chart 17.1 The number of workplaces with recent increases in flexible labour is almost offset by the number cutting back

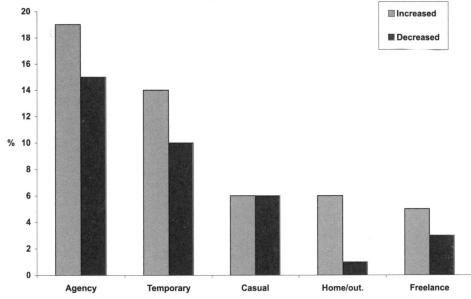

Source: Michael White, Stephen Hill, Colin Mills & Deborah Smeaton, *Managing to Change?*, Basingstoke: Palgrave, 2004, p. 32.

Significantly, the proportion of workplaces expecting to employ more people in these categories of flexible labour was far less than the number expecting to increase their workers overall (Chart 17.2). Plans for recruitment were biased toward non-flexible types of labour.

---

[2] Michael White, Stephen Hill, Colin Mills & Deborah Smeaton, *Managing to Change?*, Basingstoke: Palgrave, *2004*, p. 25.

Chart 17.2 *The number of workplaces expecting to increase their use of flexible labour is much less than the number expecting to increase workers overall*

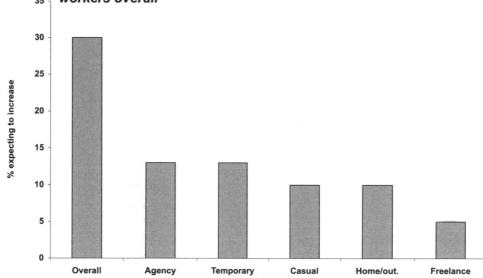

Source: Michael White, Stephen Hill, Colin Mills & Deborah Smeaton, *Managing to Change?*, Basingstoke: Palgrave, 2004, p. 32.

Figures for temporary employment point in a similar direction. The total moved up from 1.29 million in 1992 to 1,768,000 in 1997, but sank back to 1.5 million in 2004. As a proportion of all employees, temporary employment has nosed down to 6.1% from its peak of 7.8% in 1997 (Chart 17.3).

Chart 17.3 *Temporary employment (UK, seasonally adjusted, 000's, % all employees)*

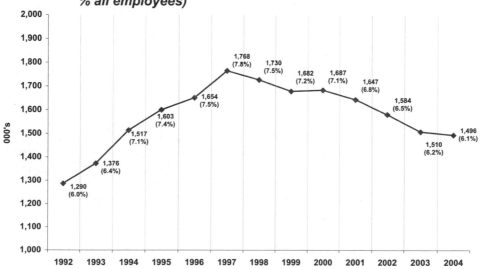

Source: ONS Labour Market Statistics – Integrated FR LFS TIME PERIODS, Tables YCBZ, MGRN.

Flexibility for employees remains limited. Chart 17.4 shows that fixed rather than flexible working hours remain dominant in the workplace. Flexi-time is the basic arrangement at only one in seven workplaces, while hardly any non-managers can choose their starting and finishing times. In the 2000 survey of employees, a mere fifth said they worked a flexible hours system, and only a further tenth (mainly managers and professionals) claimed they could decide when to start and finish.[3]

Chart 17.4 Characteristic working time arrangements in surveyed workplaces, 2002

Note: Column percentages are weighted by employment.

Source: Michael White, Stephen Hill, Colin Mills & Deborah Smeaton, *Managing to Change?,* p. 110.

Nevertheless, within this rigid framework employees have enjoyed some increase in flexibility. A few years ago most workers found it very difficult to switch from full-time to part-time employment and back again. Often they would have to move employers to do so.

But things have got better. Of establishments with part-time workers in the 2002 survey, three in five allowed transfer in both directions, and a few more permitted transfer from full-time to part-time work, though not the other way.[4] The right of parents with children under age six, and disabled children under age 18, to request flexible work since April 2003 has further increased the opportunities for parents to work part-time, or to start work earlier or finish later.

---

[3] Michael White, Stephen Hill, Colin Mills & Deborah Smeaton, *op. cit.,* p. 110.
[4] Ibid, p. 110.

The right to request part-time work has been reflected in some expansion of this form of employment – the increase in 2003 probably anticipated the legislative change. Over a longer period, however, the trend has been more stable. Though the number of part-timers has continued to rise, the proportion has stayed at roughly a quarter of all employees since the mid 1990s. Recently, the largest relative growth has been among men (Chart 17.5).

Not all part-time work reflects the employment preferences of individuals. For some it is the only work they can get.[5] But for the majority, part-time is a preferred alternative to full-time employment.

Chart 17.5 Employees in part-time work (UK, seasonally adjusted, 000's, % of all)

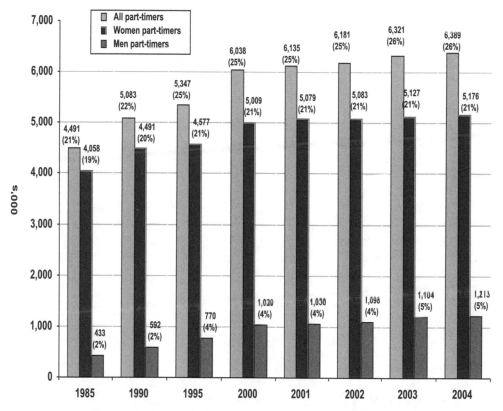

Source: ONS Labour Market Statistics – Integrated FR LFS TIME PERIODS, Tables YCBH, YCBJ, YCBN, YCBP.

---

[5] The share of part-time workers (including the self-employed) who said they wanted a full-time job increased from just over 11% in 1992 to nearly 13% in 1997. Trades Union Congress, *Things have got better – labour market performance 1992-2002,* London: TUC, 2003, p. 3.

The next 20 years

Workers will continue to want more flexibility to work the hours that suit them. This will include the freedom to work part-time for a while, to work flexible hours, to avoid unsocial hours and to take unpaid leave. But as now, employees will also be prepared to compromise on this 'wish list'.

The great majority will be willing to take full-time jobs, often with little flexibility, because they need the money or find the work intrinsically satisfying. Friendships at work cushion the discomfort of working longer hours than you want. MORI research shows that for those working long hours, social life and work is more closely entwined than for other workers.[6]

In particular, couples with young children will continue to make compromises. A survey undertaken between 1999 and 2003 found that nearly two-fifths (37.7%) of mothers with three-year old children would prefer that they and their partners both worked part-time and shared the childcare part-time. Yet in practice, 35% of the sample were doing no paid work and 47% were working part-time, while their partners were generally employed full-time.[7]

In future, might a growing number of young parents compromise on the basis of both partners working full-time? This might be driven by higher consumer expectations (to travel, for instance), the need to pay off student loans, the cost of housing as supplies remain tight and demand continues to rise, and a larger number of better-educated women reluctant to jeopardise their careers.

Research consistently shows that older workers value both choice in deciding when to retire, and the opportunity to phase their exit from employment by scaling down their work.[8] This desire for flexibility will grow as the number of 75 year olds and above increases (possibly by 75% between 2001 and 2031[9]), adding to the care responsibilities of relatives with jobs.

Yet despite their preferences, many older workers will continue to accept inflexible, full-time jobs so that they can build up a pension, pay off their mortgages and meet other financial obligations. Again, what individuals want will be tempered by the reality of their financial circumstances.

---

[6] 'Making sense of a Workaholic Society' in *Understanding Society,* London: MORI, Winter/Spring 2005.

[7] Diane M. Houston & Gillian Marks, 'Working, Caring and Sharing: Work-Life Dilemmas in Early Motherhood' in Diane M. Houston (ed.), *Work-Life Balance in the 21ˢᵗ Century,* Basingstoke: Palgrave, 2005, p. 90.

[8] For example, Sarah Vickerstaff, John Baldock, Jennifer Cox & Linda Keen, *Happy retirement? The impact of employers' policies and practice on the process of retirement,* Bristol: Policy Press, 2004, pp. 18-35.

[9] This would take the total from 4,418,000 in 2001 to 7,675,000 in 2031. *Population Trends*, 118, London: Office of National Statistics, 2004, p. 12.

All in all, workers' preferences will influence the terms on which jobs are made available in the years ahead, but they are unlikely to be the strongest driver.

Constraints on employers will be a bigger influence. The largest of these constraints will be customer expectations in the emerging 24/7 society. In four Scottish call centres staff worked variable shifts, they came in at evenings and weekends, and nearly a third took work home occasionally, all in response to customer demands.[10]

This constraint will bite more deeply as back office jobs are offshored or automated and resources are concentrated on the customer interface, where more and more value will be added. In the service economy, flexibility for consumers will take priority over flexibility for employees.

Job redesign to give workers more choice of hours will often be difficult. Cost pressures will prevent some organisations from making resources available. Introducing new processes and other priorities will come first. Middle managers will be reluctant to take risks – 'will reorganising the job work?' 'If we do it for you, will we have to do it for everyone else?' Many managers will lack the imagination and expertise.

Tight labour markets will force some employers to concede demands for part-time work, but will encourage others to resist, as we have seen. Extending part-time work might make skill shortages worse – the employer might have to recruit someone else to do the rest of the job. Allowing a highly valued employee to work part-time might spark similar demands from others, whose skills were also in short supply.

The spread of mobile and home-working may offer most hope of increasing flexibility for workers – more people will be able to mix and match work and home to suit their circumstances. But employees will not always find these options attractive. When home-working was mooted by a local authority, most staff were not keen and feared it could be isolating.[11] Work can spill over into the domestic sphere and intrude on other activities.

Typically, mobile and home-working are introduced because of the benefits they bring to the employer, such as lower office costs and the greater ability to service clients. The organisation can become more flexible, but employees may experience new forms of inflexibility: responding to work demands at inconvenient times may force them to work when they don't want to.

---

[10] Jeff Hyman, Dora Scholarios & Chris Baldry, '"Daddy, I don't like these shifts you're working because I never see you": Coping Strategies for Home and Work' in Diane M. Houston (ed.), *Work-Life Balance in the 21ˢᵗ Century,* Basingstoke: Palgrave, 2005, pp. 132-5.
[11] Stephanie Tailby, Mike Richardson, Andy Danford, Paul Stewart & Martin Upchurch, 'Workplace Partnership and Work-Life Balance: A Local Government Case Study' in Diane M. Houston (ed.), *Work-Life Balance in the 21ˢᵗ Century,* Basingstoke: Palgrave, 2005, p. 204.

Public policy will be an important driver – and could go in three directions:

> • Policy could strengthen the caring role of parents with children and adults with dependent relatives by extending flexible employment, so that family members have more time to care.

> • It could encourage paid forms of care to maximise labour force participation – one minder looking after four children allows four parents to work.

> • It could combine both these approaches to maximise employers' and employees' choice and flexibility.

UK policy ostensibly falls into the third category, but may well increasingly move toward the second one. The government proposes gradually to extend paid maternity leave to a year, with the option of fathers taking some of the leave instead. In due course, government is also highly likely to extend the right to request part-time work to older workers.

However, low levels of maternity and paternity pay will almost certainly limit the take-up of longer parental leave, while the right to request part-time work could well have only a small impact on older workers: employers may come up with legally valid reasons for saying 'no'.

Attention is likely to focus on enabling children and elderly relatives to be cared for while family members remain at work. Current initiatives are building a presumption that the state has a major responsibility for childcare. The political rhetoric is changing, with more emphasis on the contribution of high-quality care to child development. To meet the competitive challenge from the Far East, the government has called for all children aged 3 to 19 to be in some form of education.[12] Childcare is now about much more than helping parents to work.

Government intends that 15 hours of free nursery care will be available to all children aged three and four for 38 weeks of the year. When children start school at age five, 'wraparound' care will be available at either end of the school day and in the holidays.[13]

These aspirations will take some time to realise, and even then will leave considerable holes. What will happen in the child's second year, when childcare remains particularly expensive because of high staff to child ratios? For school-age children, how much will parents have to contribute to the costs of 'wraparound' care?

---

[12] *Opportunity for all: The strength to take the long-term decisions for Britain,* Pre-Budget Report, London: The Stationery Office, 2004, p. 93.
[13] A survey of 1,100 schools for 4Children found that 47% had breakfast clubs, 39% offered activities in school holidays and 34% has after-school clubs. *The Times,* 9 Sept. 2004.

In the long-term, given the present thrust of policy, state support for childcare is likely to be extended further, paid for by increased revenue from economic growth. As the state bears more of the burden, the costs of childcare for parents will gradually fall.

In 2003 the average annual cost of a full-time day nursery place was around £6,500, and around £6,000 for childminders.[14] For many parents, especially with two or more young children, these costs wipe away many of the attractions of employment. Increasing subsidies for care – whether of children or elderly relatives – will make employment a stronger option.

But will this approach be derailed by a shortage of carers? Current shortages, already acute in some areas,[15] are set to worsen as more young people go to university and then settle some distance from their parents. Less able to rely on informal care, parents (and workers with dependent relatives) will bid up the rates of paid care. A larger elderly population will require more carers.

Government will probably respond by encouraging temporary workers from abroad, and perhaps by paying grants to grandparents who have left the labour force but register as childminders.[16] The aim would be to boost both the number of women in employment and the proportion working full-time, to ease skill shortages.

Employment options for parents would remain limited, as more and more mothers were channelled into full-time work. But will the supply of overseas carers be sufficient?

Employers will want new kinds of flexibility. A growing number will move up the value chain to meet international competition and satisfy more demanding consumers, including the users of public services. They will improve product quality and introduce new offerings rather than simply reduce costs – there are limits to cost-cutting when your competitors are upgrading their products.

To compete in higher-value markets, organisations will require more highly trained employees who can work in more flexible ways – not just multi-task, rotate round jobs and cover for absent colleagues, but exercise discretion, take on extra responsibilities, do the job in a new way and improve their skills.

---

[14] Mark Ambler, David Armstrong & John Hawksworth, *Universal childcare provision in the UK – towards a cost-benefit analysis,* London: PricewaterhouseCoopers, 2003, p. 10.

[15] Costs of a nursery place in England for a child over two are reported to have risen by 7.3% between 2003 and 2004, well ahead of pay rises in general. London and the South East were hardest hit, with the cost of a place soaring by more than 17% in inner London. *The Times,* 27 January 2005.

[16] The requirement to have left the labour force, signalled possibly by a period out of employment, would be designed to prevent older workers quitting their jobs prematurely when government will be wanting them to stay on.

Already this is starting to happen. About half the workplaces surveyed in 2002 had asked some of their employees to undertake a greater variety of tasks in the previous three years. The same proportion had given increased training to cover for other jobs. Three in ten had extended their use of job rotation systems, in which employees take on different jobs at different times.[17]

Team working, which extends flexibility in other ways, has been expanding steadily. Over one half of employees said they worked in a group in 2000, up by 10% since 1992. Three in ten workplaces said they were increasing the use of formal teams, with hardly any moving in the opposite direction.[18]

'The policy of intelligent flexibility', which expects employees to work in more intelligent ways, 'is forging ahead much more rapidly than the policy of buying in flexible labour.'[19] But the two are not alternatives: both are so widespread that they appear to be complementary, perhaps even reinforcing each other. The conditions that give rise to the one encourage the other.

Might 'intelligent flexibility' begin to spread at the expense of traditional forms of flexibility? As now, intelligent flexibility will require training, which will mean long-term investment in people. Employers will not want to write this investment off by continually hiring and firing staff.

Nor as they move up the value chain may they want to rely on skilled contract labour, perhaps obtained from an agency. In tight labour markets, they will want to know that their supply is secure and avoid a bidding war among workers whose skills are scarce. As it becomes more high-tech, for example, might an organisation keep its computer programmers in house, to be certain they understand the peculiarities of the system?

Although many employers will prefer to hang on to their staff and work them more intelligently, this will not apply to everyone. In 'hour-glass' Britain, other employers will stick to low-skilled activities at the cheaper end of the domestic market, and value traditional flexibility in obtaining and dispensing with labour.

Yet as prosperity trickles down to the bottom of the glass and increases the demand for higher quality offerings at even this end of the market, might some of these low-cost employers be forced to upgrade their processes and work in more intelligent ways too?

What might be the implications?

Flexibility for employers may be slowly redefined, with traditional forms of labour market flexibility giving way to intelligent flexibility. Rather than relying on external flexibility in the labour market, such as the ability to recruit temporary or contract workers, employers may seek greater internal flexibility among their workers instead.

---

[17] Michael White, Stephen Hill, Colin Mills & Deborah Smeaton, *op. cit.,* p. 41.

[18] Ibid, p. 45.

[19] Ibid, p. 43.

Today's talk about flexible labour markets could become increasingly out of date. The key to competitiveness would lie not in having a flexible labour market as we understand it today, but in employers' ability to introduce smarter methods of work. What might be implications for public policy?

Flexibility for employees may also be redefined, especially for parents. The demand for support in combining work and children looks likely to be met through the extension of childcare, rather than mainly through greater freedom to work part-time or perhaps flexi-hours.

This would reduce one set of options for women, but open up other opportunities. Mothers would have more chance of staying in a full-time job, with the advantages of salary and career progression that this can bring. Might the benefits of this alternative freedom, the freedom to advance in your career, be taken for granted in 20 years' time?

Three patterns of work-life balance could emerge: [20]

- A 'blended' future may exist, especially for the growing numbers who work at home for some of the time and on the move. Work and home could become more joined-up, as individuals jump back and forth between the two. But will individuals have the skills and discipline to manage parallel worlds, so that the two do not collide uncomfortably?

- A 'balanced' future may eventually – perhaps – be in reach of more workers than today. Employees working full-time would keep home and work apart. A progressive increase in state help with child and elder-care would help workers to be more fulfilled in both. But faced with the shortage of carers, will governments be able to keep care affordable?

- A 'battered' future looks set to continue, at least in the medium term. Today's tension between work and home will persist, as gaps in the government's childcare proposals leave workers struggling to combine work with children. The struggle may continue if guest workers from overseas and 'granny care' fail to keep down the costs of looking after children.

These alternatives will have implications for well-being. Individuals' well-being is strongly linked with appropriate levels of autonomy. Not enough control over your life can leave you feeling frustrated and inadequate: control over too much can make you anxious. Clearly, keeping work and life in balance is vital for the sense of being in control – of being able to cope. If for no other reason, this will keep work-life balance high on the political agenda.

---

[20] These possibilities are discussed more fully in Michael Moynagh and Richard Worsley, *Tomorrow's Workplace. Fulfilment or stress?*, King's Lynn: The Tomorrow Project, 2001, pp. 55-76.

Points to take away

• Flexible labour markets will become steadily less important to employers than 'intelligent flexibility' – smart methods of working that require individuals to be more flexible.

• This flexibility will be dictated more by employers' than employees' needs.

• Work-life balance will remain problematic for many parents with children. But will their interests increasingly diverge from the rest of the workforce who, as now, will be more ready to accept employers' terms?

18. Conclusion

Working in the 21st century will be complex and varied. No simple picture will emerge. It would be rash to predict the future with confidence, but the following are suggestions as to what may be in store over the next 20 years.

• New products, new processes and new technologies will transform work, as Britain moves up the value chain into activities that earn more revenue. Video-conferencing, virtual reality, powerful new search engines and other technologies will encourage smart forms of work. Jobs will become more complex, teams will multiply, and individuals and teams will be given more responsibility.

• Jobs will grow in the 'aesthetic' economy, which has been the second fastest generator of jobs in London after business services. As low-cost manufactures flood the market from abroad, companies will earn income not through making, but through designing and marketing. Profits will lie in products that make a fashion statement and appeal to the senses. Entertainment and consumption will merge.

• Money will increasingly be made at the customer interface. The proliferation of mentors, personal trainers, lifestyle advisers, style consultants and concierge services herald new forms of personalised customer support, which will create many jobs. As their tasks are automated, for example, supermarket check-out staff may become shopping advisers.

• The 'jobs gap' will be the new priority. Over the next 20 years, 'hour-glass' Britain will see good jobs at the top pulling away from 'Mcjobs' at the bottom. Fewer jobs will exist in the middle. Getting a job will not be enough to escape poverty: finding 'good' work will be vital. Today's strategy of reducing poverty through helping the unemployed into work may be eclipsed by a new emphasis: narrowing the divide between good and bad jobs.

• The demand for 'social capital' skills will grow as employees pool knowledge, work collaboratively and relate closely to customers. Skills like 'listening carefully to colleagues' are becoming central to work. Companies will thrive on good company, forcing schools to pay more attention to interpersonal skills. Emotional literacy may one day be part of the core curriculum.

• Many workers will find themselves in a sellers' market. Employers will be strapped for skills, and fewer young people will be entering the workforce. Organisations will look to older people, migrant workers and people who have left employment to meet their needs, but none of these sources of labour will be sufficient on their own, and even together they may be inadequate. Employers will tackle workplace stress with new urgency to cut absenteeism, prevent sickness and keep key workers healthy.

• Barriers to gender equality at work will fall, more women will work full-time and the number of women earning more than their partners will grow slowly. More women as the main breadwinner could eventually bring changes to society every bit as radical as the initial influx of women to work.

• Self-employment is unlikely to accelerate. The challenge will to encourage more entrepreneurship within organisations.

• The end of 'jobs for life' is a myth. The average time people spend in a job has actually increased. Almost 95% of men work in a permanent job. The proportion of workers seeing themselves as having a career jumped from just under half in 1985 to over 60% in 2001. Long-term, full-time jobs will be far more typical than portfolio working and temporary employment. Employers who invest in knowledge workers will want to hang on to their staff.

• There will be dramatic changes in how people work. Today over five million people, almost a fifth of employees, spend some time working from home or on the move. Mobile workers, who work in a hotel, an airport lounge or a motorway service station, will be one of the fastest growing groups of employees. New techniques to manage these workers will transform how employees are supervised.

• Organisations will turn on their heads as workers at the bottom lead innovation – but this development will come slowly. In time, managers at the top will no longer be the prime leaders of change: they will design sophisticated networks that link up individuals and enable others to take the lead. Being at the top will be about designing, managing and repairing these networks. New methods of combining control with radical decentralisation will make this transformation possible.

• Outsourcing to British-based suppliers will be limited, though offshoring will expand steadily. Some activities will be outsourced, but others will be brought back in-house so that managers can keep control. Employers will be more discerning in what they outsource and what they don't.

• League tables and target-setting will be revolutionised. Measuring the capacity to learn and improve will replace crude measurements of output.

• Some organisations will align incentive pay more closely to elements that are vital for performance. Others will move away from incentive pay altogether. Pay packages will include help with paying off the mortgage, new savings schemes and the choice between longer holidays and higher pay.

• Trade unions are unlikely to make a strong come-back. New forms of employee involvement will spread, often driven by changes in employment law, and workers will become more litigious.

• Workers will be entitled to more holidays and to work fewer hours each week. But more people will ignore these entitlements and bring work home in the evening or take their laptops on holiday. To overcome skill shortages, government will prioritise better childcare to free up mothers to work full-time.

• Flexible labour markets, traditionally understood, will become less important to employers than 'intelligent flexibility' – smart methods of working that require individuals to be more adaptable. This flexibility will be dictated more by the needs of employers than workers.

Finding a conceptual framework for these developments remains a challenge to researchers in the field. However, four themes tie many of the changes together:

• Moving up the value chain will create new types of employment and transform how people work.

• Tight labour markets will encourage employers to search for new sources of skill, develop policies to retain labour and listen to their workers carefully.

• Changes in how people work will be more significant than in how they are employed. Jobs for life are not about to disappear, for example, but we shall see more mobile forms of work.

• New forms of management will include innovative approaches to reward, to measuring performance and to encourage 'responsible' workers, who will use their greater autonomy to promote the organisation's goals.

Taken together, these developments will revolutionise work. But because most changes will be incremental and people will be more used to change, the revolution will feel like evolution.

Selected bibliography

14-19 Education and Skills, cm 6476, London: The Stationery Office, 2005.

Bayliss, V, *Redefining Work: An RSA Initiative,* London: RSA, 1998.

Bradley, B., Healy, G. & Mukherjee, N., 'Inclusion, Exclusion and Separate Organisation – Black Women Activists in Trade Unions', *Future of Work Series Working Paper 25,* Leeds: ESRC Future of Work Programme, 2002.

Brown, W., Marginson, P. & Walsh, J., 'The Management of Pay as the Influence of Collective Bargaining Diminishes' in Paul Edwards (ed.), *Industrial Relations. Theory and Practice,* Oxford: Blackwell, 2003.

Brown, W., & Oxenbridge, S., 'Trade Unions and Collective Bargaining: Law and The Future of Collectivism' in Catherine Barnard, Simon Deakin and Gill Morris, (eds.) *The Renewal of Labour Law*, 2003

Coleman, D., 'Demographic, economic and social consequences of UK migration 'in Disney, H. (ed.), *Work in Progress. Migration, Integration and the European Labour Market*, London: Civitas, 2003.

Controlling our borders: Making migration work for Britain. Five year strategy for asylum and immigration, cm 6472, London: The Stationery Office, 2005.

Cooper, C. L. (ed.), *Leadership and Management in the 21st Century,* Oxford: OUP, 2005.

Cully, M., Woodland, S., O'Reilly A. & Dix, G., *Britain at Work,* London: Routledge, 1999.

Department for Work and Pensions Five Year Strategy. Opportunity and security throughout life, cm 6447, London: the Stationery Office, 2005.

Dex, S. & Smith, C., *The nature and pattern of family-friendly employment policies in Britain,* Bristol: Policy Press, 2002.

Dickens, R., Gregg, P., & Wadsworth, J., *The Labour Market Under New Labour. The State of Working Britain 2003,* London: Palgrave, 2003.

Dorling, D. & Thomas, B., *People and Places: A 2001 Census atlas of the UK,* Bristol: Policy Press, 2004.

Edwards, P. (ed), *Industrial Relations. Theory and Practice,* Oxford: Blackwell, 2003.

Felstead, A., Gallie, D., Green, F., *Work Skills in Britain 1986-2001,* DfES, 2002.

Felstead, A., Jewson, N. & Walters, S., 'The Changing Place of Work', *Future of Work Series, Working Paper 28,* Leeds: ESRC Future of Work Programme, n.d.

Felstead, A., Jewson, N., & Walters, S., *Changing Places of Work,* Basingstoke: Palgrave, 2005.

Fuller, T., 'If you wanted to know the future of small business what questions would you ask', *Futures*, 35(4), 2003.

Glover, S., Gott, C., Loizillon, A., Portes, J., Price R., Spencer, S., Srinivason V. & Willis, C., *Migration: an economic and social analysis*, RDS Occasional Paper No. 67, London: Home Office, 2001.

Green, F. & McIntosh, S., *Working on the Chain Gang? An Examination of Rising Effort Levels in Europe in the 1990s*, London: LSE Centre for Economic Performance, Discussion Paper 465, 2000.

Healy, G., Bradley, H. & Mukherjee, N., 'Getting In – Getting Active: The Experience of Minority Ethnic Women in Trade Unions', *Future of Work Series – Working Paper 29*, Leeds: ESRC Future of Work Programme, 2003.

Healy, G., Heery, E., Taylor, P. & Brown, W., *The Future of Worker Representation*, Basingstoke: Palgrave, 2004.

Heery, E., 'The trade union response to agency labour in Britain', *Industrial Relations Journal*, 35(5), 2004.

Heery, E., Conley, H., Delbridge, R., & Stewart, P., 'Beyond Enterprise? Trade Unions and the Representation of Contingent Workers', *Future of Work Series – Working Paper 7*, Leeds: ESRC Future of Work Programme, n.d.

Heery, E., Simms, M., Conley, H., Delbridge, R. & Stewart, P., 'Trade Unions and the Flexible Workforce: A Survey Analysis of Union Policy and Practice', *Future of Work Series – Working Paper 22*, Leeds: Future of Work Programme, 2002.

HM Treasury, *Long-term global economic challenges and opportunities for the UK*, London: The Stationery Office, 2004.

Houston, D. M. (ed.), *Work-Life Balance in the 21st Century*, Basingstoke: Palgrave, 2005.

Improving the Life Chances of Disabled People, London: The Prime Minister's Strategy Unit, 2005.

Institute for Employment Research, *Projections of Occupations and Qualifications 1999/2000*, Coventry and London: University of Warwick & DfEE, 2000.

Keep, E., Mayhew, K., Corney, M., *Review of the Evidence on the Rate of Return to Employers of Investment in Training and Employer Training Measures*, London: DTI, 2002.

Macaulay, C., 'Job mobility and job tenure in the UK', *Labour Market Trends*, 111(11), 2003.

McOrmond, T., 'Changes in working trends over the past decade', *Labour Market Trends*, 112(1), 2004.

Moynagh, M. & Worsley, R., *Learning from the future: Scenarios for post-16 learning*, London: Learning & Skills Research Centre, 2003.

Moynagh, M. & Worsley, R., *The Opportunity of a Lifetime: Reshaping Retirement*, London: CIPD, 2004.

Munro, A. & Rainbird, H., 'Opening doors as well as banging on tables: an assessment of UNISON/employer partnerships on learning in the UK public sector', *Industrial Relations Journal*, 35(5), 2004.

Nolan, P., & Slater, G., 'The Labour Market: History, Structure and Prospects' in Paul Edwards (ed), *Industrial Relations. Theory and Practice*, Oxford: Blackwell, 2003

Nolan, P., & Wood, S., 'Mapping the Future of Work', *British Journal of Industrial Relations*, 41(2), 2003.

O'Connell, A., *Raising State Pension Age: Are We Ready?*, London: Pensions Policy Institute, 2002.

Part-time is no crime – so why the penalty?, London: Equal Opportunities Commission, 2005.

Pensions: Challenges and Choices. The First Report of the Pensions Commission, London: The Stationery Office, 2004.

Reward management 2003, London: Chartered Institute of Personnel & Development, 2003.

Reward management: Annual survey report 2005, London: Chartered Institute of Personnel & Development, 2005.

Rifkin, J., *The End of Work*, New York: Putnam, 1995.

Sennett, R., *The Corrosion of Character*, New York: W. W. Norton, 1998

Stewart, P. (ed.), *Employment, Trade Union Renewal and the Future of Work*, Basingstoke: Palgrave, 2004.

Tailby, S., Richardson, M., Stewart, P., Danford, A. & Upchurch, M., 'Partnership at work and worker participation: an NHS case study', *Industrial Relations Journal*, 35(5), 2004.

Taylor, R., *Diversity in Britain's Labour Market*, ESRC Future of Work Seminar Series, Swindon: ESRC, 2003.

Taylor, R., *Managing Workplace Change*, ESRC Future of Work Programme Seminar Series, Swindon: ESRC, n.d.

Taylor, R., *Partnerships at Work. The Way to Corporate Renewal?*, ESRC Future of Work Programme Seminar Series, Swindon: ESRC, 2004.

Taylor, R., *Skills and Innovation in Modern Workplaces*, ESRC Future of Work Programme Seminar Series, Swindon: ESRC, 2003.

Taylor, R., *The Future of Employment Relations*, ESRC Future of Work Seminar Series, Swindon: ESRC, 2003.

Trades Union Congress, *Things have got better – labour market performance 1992-2002*, London: TUC, 2003.

Vickerstaff, S., Baldock, J., Cox, J. & Keen, L., *Happy retirement? The impact of employers' policies and practice on the process of retirement,* Bristol: Policy Press, 2004.

Welfare to Work: Tackling the Barriers to the Employment of Older People, Report by the Comptroller and Auditor General, London: The Stationery Office, 2004.

White, M., Hill, S., Mills, C. & Smeaton, D., *Managing to Change?,* Basingstoke: Palgrave, 2004.

Willmott, M. & Nelson, W., *Complicated Lives,* London: Wiley, 2003.

Wittington, R. & Mayer, M., *Organising for Success in the Twenty-First Century,* London: Chartered Institute of Personnel & Development, 2002.

Wolf, A., *Does Education Matter?* London: Penguin, 2002.

Zuboff, S. & Maxmin, J., *The Support Economy,* London: Allen Lane, 2003.

Index

Activity allowances 65
Advanced economies 18, 23
'Aesthetic economy' 29, 183
Affluence 167
Africa 57
Age discrimination 43, 44
Ageing population 37, 54
Agency work/workers 94-5, 180
Amicus 151
Apprenticeships 45
ASDA 132
Asia 12, 15, 32, 51
Associate professionals 11
Asylum seekers 53
Authoritarian leadership 134
Automation 10-11, 16, 21, 105, 111-12
Autonomy 130-31, 134-6

B&Q 156
Baby boom generation 43
Bank of England 14
'Bottom-up' culture 131-2
'Boundary-less organisations' 118
BP 112-13
'Brain drain' 57
Britain at Work Survey (1992) 95
British Household Panel Survey 171-2
Built environment 109

Capita 119
Capital-intensive production 22
Career progression 96
Carers 178-9
Change in Employer
Practices Survey (2002) 102
Change management 98, 117, 120
Chartered Inst. of Personnel and
Development (CIPD) 137, 138, 139, 141, 142
Childcare 79, 81-2, 176, 178-9
City and Guilds 41, 45
Collaborative
networks 112
skills 136
Collective bargaining 149, 150, 153, 154
Communications technologies 89-90, 103,
105, 116

Community development 31
Competition 114-15, 168
Competitive advantage 119
Conglomerates 123
Consumer expectations 117
Corporate
decision-making 115, 134
power 88-9
Customer-facing
organisations 116-17, 177, 183
skills 98
staff 145
Customisation 111, 112, 116-17, 130

Davignon report 158
Decentralisation 120-21
Declining industries 29
Degree-level jobs 21
Delegation 116, 127-8, 129
Demographics 16-17
Department for Education 120-21
Department of Work and Pensions 66
Dependents 48
Developed economics 49-50
Developing economies 15, 56-7
Direct contribution (DC) pension schemes 146
Disadvantaged groups 64-9
Diversity 55-6, 80

Early years development 68-9
Earnings gap 19-20, 23-4, 76-7, 81, 146
Eastern European migrants 52
Economies of scale 122
Economy 13-15
Education
best practice 120-21
disadvantaged children 69
emerging economies 50
extensions to 40
improvements 51
key skills 32-3
women 78
Education Maintenance Allowances 65, 66
Egalitarian societies 23
Electronic networks 89-90
Emerging economies 15, 50
Emotional literacy 30, 33

'Employability' 91
Employee
       consultation 151-2, 156-7, 158
       flexibility 171-2, 174-5, 178, 181
Employer flexibility 171-2, 176-7, 178,
          179-81
Employer-based training 31-2, 91-2
Employers Skills Survey (2001) 22
Employment
       contracts 4
       growth 153
       numbers 11
       rates 37-9, 44, 60-61, 73-4
       stability 95
       trends by occupation/sector 8-10
       types by gender 93-4
Employment Relations Act (1999) 149
Employment Service 61
Empowerment 127-36
Entrepreneurship 89, 91
Equal opportunities 76-7, 82, 155
Equal Opportunities Commission 71, 76
Equal Pay Act (1975) 71
Ethnic minorities 52, 55-6
       employment rates 60-61
European Commission 158
European Court of Justice 151
European Survey on Working Conditions 129
European Union (EU) 15, 52, 71, 78, 129,
          132, 151
       Directives 43, 151, 156, 157, 164, 165
Exchange rates 15

Family-friendly policies 17, 18, 75, 155
Final salary pensions 42
Financial
       controls 121
       rewards 139-40
       stability 97
Flexi-hours 181
Flexible
       labour markets 133, 171-82, 185
       remuneration systems 155
       working practices 75
Foreign remittances 51, 56-7
Free-riders 154
Freelance employment/workers 98, 172
Fulfilment 135
Full-time employment 18, 93-4, 103, 176
Future Foundation 44

Future Work Forum 108

Gender
       employment types 93-4
       equality/power 75-6, 78-80, 82, 184
       segregation 72-3
Gershon review 21, 66
Global
       competition 168
       economic growth 12-13
Grading structures 113-14, 122, 144
Graduate apprenticeships 45
Graduates 97

Health and Safety Executive 63, 130, 135
Henley Management Centre 108
Hierarchical organisations 121-2
High-value
       jobs 17, 21, 121
       markets 179-80
Higher education 32-3, 40-41, 50, 78
Holiday entitlements 165-6, 185
Home-workers/working 101-9, 172, 177
'Hot-desking' 102, 107
'Hour-glass' 2, 19, 20, 22, 25, 180, 183
Hours of work 163-9
Household chores 81-2
Housing 53, 109
Human interactions 10-11
Human resource management (HRM) 80,
          119, 122, 132-3, 143-4, 157

Illegal immigrants 53, 56
Illness 61, 62-4
Immigration 47-9
       responses to 52-3
In-sourcing 89, 119
Inactivity 59-69
Incapacity benefits 59, 61, 62, 63, 64, 67
Incentives
       for change 133
       to work 42, 45, 66
Indentured labour 56
Individual learning accounts 91
Individualisation 91
Industrial tribunals 155
Inflation 144
Informal economy 56

Information rights 156-7
Information technology (IT) 104, 105, 112,
                                116, 121
Institute of Management 106
'Intelligent flexibility' 180, 185
Interpersonal
        skills 30
        work 16, 105-6
'Intrapreneurs' 89

Job
        coaching 64
        content 96, 99
        gap 183
        numbers 7-18
        polarisation 22-4
        quality 19-25
        redesign 177
        rotation 180
        segregation 72-3, 80
        stability 90, 95, 97-8
'Jobs for life' 93-100, 184
Jobseeker's Allowance 61, 64

Key
        skills 32-3
        staff 98
Knowledge
        accumulation 97-8
        transfer 106
        work/workers 24, 89-90, 142, 145
Knowledge-intensive sectors 13, 29, 97

Labour
        demand 40-41
        supply 54-5, 81
Labour Force Survey 94, 95, 102
Labour market 22-4
        see also tight labour markets
Labour-intensive jobs 9, 16
Leadership styles 133-4
LearnDirect 65
Learning
        organisations 131
        partnerships 158
Leisure 107
Life skills 30-31
Lifestyle preferences 75-6, 79

Location of Work Survey (2002) 104
LogicaCMG 119
London School of Economics 10
'Long hours culture' 164
Long-term illness 43, 61, 67
Low-cost employers/jobs 8, 133, 180
Low income households 68
Low-paid workers 144
Low-skilled jobs 50, 61

Management
        capacity 132-3
        of change 98, 117-18
        control 108, 134-5
        de-layering 113
        grades 114, 122
        motivational forms 4
        of time 108
Managers
        number 113
        women as 77, 82
Manpower 95, 153
Manufacturing
        import prices 14
        jobs 17
Marks and Spencer 112
Maternity rights 75, 178
Mediation 156
Men
        activity 73
        inactivity 59-61
Mental illness 61, 62-4, 65-6
Menu-based reward packages 144, 168
Micro-companies 86-8, 91
Migrant workers 47-58, 179
Migration 51-2
Migration Watch UK 48
Mobile work 103, 105-6, 107, 108, 109,
                168, 177, 184
'Modular corporations' 118
Monitoring devices 132
MORI 176
Mothers 73-5
Motivational forms of management 4

National Health Service (NHS) 63, 64, 115,
                                119, 156
National Minimum Wage 17, 22, 24, 62, 67-8,
                        80, 144, 145, 146

National skills surveys 27-8
'Network organisations' 118
Networking 90, 112
New Deal 62, 64
'New' economy 24, 28-9
Non-permanent jobs 94-5

Occupational pensions 45
Office space 104, 106
'Offshoring' 20-21, 112, 113, 119, 168, 184
Ofsted 131
'Old' economy skills 29
Older workers 37-46, 167, 176
'Open plan' offices 101
Organisational
        change 111-23, 184
        form 118-19
        values 145
'Out of hours' working 168-9
Outsourcing 88, 112-13, 119-20, 122, 184

Parenting 69, 79, 189
Part-time employment
        older people 39, 176
        practicality 167
        right to request 174-5, 181
        students 18, 41
        women 72
Participation measures 67-9
Partnership agreements 155-6
Paternity rights 75, 178
'Pathways to Work' 64
Pay
        agreements 154
        structures 140
Pensions 38, 42, 44-5, 146
Performance
        appraisals 135, 143
        management 130-31
        related pay 141-4
Personal
        development 136
        identity 99-100
        services 87-8, 116
Personalised
        reward systems 144, 145
        spaces/time 107
        support 66
Pirelli 129

Pizza Express 156
Points system of immigration 53
Poverty 24
Prime Minister's Strategy Unit 68
Prince's Trust 88
'Process-based organisations' 119
Production strategies 22
'Project-based organisations' 118
Public
        sector 17, 42, 135, 145, 150
        service 114-15

Qualifications
        older people 39
        trends 22, 28
        younger people 62
'Quality circles' 127, 128
Quality of jobs 19-25

Recreation products 169
Recruitment
        employers 45
        unions 153
Relationships 106
Relationships skills 30-31
Relocation 51-2, 56, 103, 109
Retail prices 14
Retention 45, 98
Retirement
        delay 18, 44-5
        mandatory 43, 44
Reward packages 17, 137-47, 184
Rifkin, Jeremy 7, 11, 18
Risk control 117
Role reversal 81-2

Sainsbury's 112
Savings schemes 145-6
Sectoral employment trends 8-10
Self-employment 39, 85-92, 184
Self-management 120, 130, 131, 142
Self-service 117
Service-related progression 141
Sex Discrimination Act (1975) 71
Shared leadership 134
Shell Livewire 88
Shift patterns 168, 169, 177

Silicon Valley 49, 169
Single parents 74
Skills
    deficiencies 22
    development 91-2
    immigrants 49
    requirements 27-34
    shortages 49, 66, 98, 144, 168
Smart systems 142
Social
    capital 30, 31, 33, 183
    exclusion 24
    inclusion 69
Statutory rights 151, 152, 155, 156-7, 174-5
Strategic
    control 128-9
    reward practices 138
Stress 23, 63, 135-6
Students 18, 41
Supervision 128-9
Supply chains 120
Sure Start 69

Target-setting 143
Task discretion 129
Tax credits 24, 62
Teacher Training Agency 49
Technologies 65, 96, 104, 105-6, 132
Temporary staff 172, 173
Thomson, Peter 108
Tight labour markets 3, 16-17, 80, 144, 177, 185
Time management 108
Top down reward systems 137-8
Total Quality programmes 129
'Total reward' approach 139, 144, 145-6
Training 31-2, 97-8, 136
Transaction costs 115, 119, 123
Transport and General Workers Union 151, 153
Transport congestion 53, 109
TUC 149

Unemployment 59-60
Unions 22, 137, 146, 149-59, 185
UNISON 158
United Nations (UN) 50
USA 49, 50, 78, 81, 85, 95

Value chain 21, 130-31, 142-3, 179-80, 185
Value-added jobs 7-8, 17, 21
Vertical organisations 121-2
Video-conferencing 103, 105, 116
'Virtual corporations' 118
Vocational
    education 33
    training 64-5

Warwick Institute for Employment Research 16
Welfare system 61-2
Well-being 181
Willetts, David 146
Women
    pensions 42
    workers 71-82
Woodward, Sir Clive 99
Work
    importance 18
    intensification 129-30
Work-life balance 77, 82, 167, 181
Working
    hours 163-9, 174
    mothers 73-5, 79, 81, 176
    practices 4, 104, 185
Working Families 75
Working in Britain Survey (2000) 95
Workplace
    culture 131-2
    development programmes 158
    environment 101-3, 106
    transformation 2-3
World Bank 13
'Wraparound' care 178

Younger people
    disadvantaged 64-7
    inactivity levels 62-3
Younger workers
    recruitment and retention 45
    supply 40-41